T0087514

Praise for *Plastic Unlimited*

'Timely, engaging, comprehensive. Mah delivers the book I've been waiting for – a power-and-geopolitics analysis of the multifaceted plastics crisis, past and present.'
Rebecca Altman, writer and environmental sociologist

'*Plastic Unlimited* uncovers the driving forces behind the global problem of plastic waste that is damaging ecosystems, undermining public health, and widening inequalities. Alice Mah's incisive analysis shows that the current plastics predicament is not mainly a problem of weak waste management or poor consumer choices, but instead is driven by powerful corporations that dominate plastics production and use.'
Jennifer Clapp, University of Waterloo

'With breathtaking originality, Alice Mah exposes why plastics are poisoning our planet. Governance is failing. And corporations are out of control. Everyone should rush to read this incisive, fiery analysis. These companies must be held accountable.'
Peter Dauvergne, University of British Columbia

'Tracing plastics back to their petrochemical source, *Plastic Unlimited* presents an unflinching investigation into corporate responsibility for the plastics crisis. Mah convincingly argues that plastics consumption and climate change are interlinked, and offers strategies for confronting these fossil-fuelled crises through multi-scalar activism.'
Jennifer Gabrys, University of Cambridge and author of *Citizens of Worlds: Open-Air Toolkits for Environmental Struggle*

Plastic Unlimited

Plastic Unlimited

How Corporations Are Fuelling
the Ecological Crisis and
What We Can Do About It

Alice Mah

polity

First published in 2022 by Polity Press

Polity Press
65 Bridge Street
Cambridge CB2 1UR, UK

Polity Press
101 Station Landing
Suite 300
Medford, MA 02155, USA

ISBN-13: 978-1-5095-4945-0
ISBN-13: 978-1-5095-4946-7 (pb)

A catalogue record for this book is available from the British Library.

Library of Congress Control Number: 2021948544

Typeset in 11 on 13 pt Sabon
by Fakenham Prepress Solutions, Fakenham, Norfolk NR21 8NL
Printed and bound in the UK by TJ Books Limited

The publisher has used its best endeavours to ensure that the URLs for external websites referred to in this book are correct and active at the time of going to press. However, the publisher has no responsibility for the websites and can make no guarantee that a site will remain live or that the content is or will remain appropriate.

Every effort has been made to trace all copyright holders, but if any have been overlooked the publisher will be pleased to include any necessary credits in any subsequent reprint or edition.

For further information on Polity, visit our website:
politybooks.com

Contents

Abbreviations

AAP	American Academy of Pediatrics
BP	British Petroleum
BPA	bisphenol A
CCS	carbon capture and storage
CIEL	Centre for International Environmental Law
COP26	UN Climate Conference (2021)
COTC	crude-oil-to-chemicals
DEHP	di(2-ethylhexyl) phthalate
EPR	Extended Producer Responsibility
ESG	environmental, social, and governance
EuPC	European Plastics Converters
FMCG	fast-moving consumer goods
GFANZ	Glasgow Financial Alliance for Net Zero
$GtCO_2e$	gigatons of carbon dioxide equivalent
HDPE	high-density polyethylene
IEA	International Energy Agency
IP	International Petroleum
IPCC	Intergovernmental Panel on Climate Change
IRENA	International Renewable Energy Agency
ISSB	International Sustainability Standards Board
LCAs	lifecycle assessments

LDPE	low-density polyethylene
LLDPE	linear low-density polyethylene
LNG	liquefied natural gas
NPRA	National Petroleum Refiners Association
OECD	Organization for Economic Cooperation and Development
OSHA	Occupational Safety and Health Administration
PET	polyethylene terephthalate
PFAS	per- and polyfluoroalkyl substances
PFOA	perfluorooctanoic acid
PLASTICS	Plastics Industry Association
PP	polypropylene
PVC	polyvinyl chloride
SBTI	Science-Based Target Initiative
UNEA	United Nations Environment Assembly
UNEP	United Nations Environment Programme
WBCSD	World Business Council for Sustainable Development

Acknowledgements

The idea for this book was sparked by reflecting on the continual expansion of global plastics production despite international efforts to tackle plastic pollution, the climate crisis, and the COVID-19 pandemic. I am grateful to Louise Knight at Polity Press for encouraging me to pursue this project and for working with me to help it take shape. I also thank the whole Polity team, particularly Inès Boxman and Justin Dyer for editorial guidance. From the beginning, I was filled with a sense of urgency at the invitation to delve deeper into the corporate roots and toxic consequences of the escalating plastics crisis.

I thank the Leverhulme Trust for providing funding to research and write this book through the Philip Leverhulme Prize. Some parts of chapter 3 are revised versions of work that was originally published in my article 'Future-Proofing Capitalism: The Paradox of the Circular Economy for Plastics', *Global Environmental Politics*, 21(2) (2021): 121–42, available open access, which received funding from the European Research Council (ERC) under the European Union's Horizon 2020 research and innovation programme (grant agreement 639583) and the Leverhulme Trust.

Many thanks to two anonymous readers of the manuscript who provided generous and constructive feedback, particularly on nuancing the early history of plastics, the analysis of corporations, and the discussion of waste colonialism. I also thank two readers of the book proposal for their valuable advice on refining the corporate focus of the project. I gratefully acknowledge Nerea Calvillo and Sandra Eckert for offering helpful comments on early drafts, and David Brown for excellent research assistance. A big thanks to the Toxic Expertise research team for collaborative insights over the years into different aspects of the complex global petrochemical industry: David Brown, Thom Davies, Lorenzo Feltrin, Patricio Flores Silva, India Holme, Calvin Jephcote, Alexandra Kviat, Loretta Lou, Thomas Verbeek, Chris Waite, and Xinhong Wang. I am also thankful for the intellectual encouragement from all of my wonderful colleagues at the Department of Sociology at the University of Warwick. The final manuscript benefited from my participation in the conference 'Global Governance of Plastic Pollution: Transforming the Global Plastics Economy' hosted by the Global Governance Centre at the Graduate Institute in Geneva and the United Nations Conference on Trade and Development (UNCTAD) in August 2021. Thanks to Diana Barrowclough, Luisa Cortat, and Carolyn Deere Birkbeck for the invitation to this timely and important event.

Thanks so much to Eric and Kathy Mah for all the support and encouragement, and to Alex, Erica, and Jennifer Mah for inspiring me through living and thinking ecologically. Thank you to Manuela Galetto, Mouzayian Khalil-Babatunde, and Nirmal Puwar for helping to get me through the intensive months of writing during the pandemic with socially distanced walks. Special thanks to Colin Stephen, who read many drafts closely and supported me and my writing in more ways than words can express. This book is dedicated to our son, Lucian, who has some great ideas about how to save the planet.

1

Plastic Unlimited

The world woke up to the global plastics crisis in 2017 and to the climate emergency in 2018. On the eve of the COVID-19 pandemic, sustainability issues were dominating plastics industry discussions due to the groundswell of public backlash. However, by spring 2020 single-use plastics were back in favour, seen as necessary to fight the virus. Plastic recycling programmes ground to a halt, their viability thrown into question as the price of crude oil plummeted. People despaired over the piles of takeaway containers and facemasks strewn over public spaces, but global attention to the wider issue had shifted. After all, plastic pollution paled in comparison with the more immediate global health crisis. The climate emergency, by contrast, gained considerable political momentum during the pandemic, as governments around the world resolved to accelerate the transition away from fossil fuels through green recoveries.

The plastics crisis is inextricably linked to crises of global heating, toxic pollution, biodiversity loss, and global inequality. It exemplifies an existential planetary threat of overconsumption beyond the sustainable limits of the earth. There are serious social and ecological consequences of sidelining plastic pollution as a lesser kind of crisis competing for bandwidth in a crisis-saturated world. The toxic impacts of plastic pollution compound existing social inequalities concentrated in climate-vulnerable coastal communities and in disadvantaged fenceline communities (i.e. communities immediately adjacent to polluting companies) around the planet. If current policies continue, plastic waste is projected to rise from 11 million tons of plastic entering the ocean per year in 2020 to 29 million tons per year by 2040. In the same period, global plastics production is forecast to use 19% of the world's total remaining carbon budget to keep global heating within the limit of 1.5 degrees.[1] Combined with the deadly heat waves, floods, mass extinctions, and pandemics that come with climate catastrophe, the world will be smothered in toxic plastic waste within the span of one generation.

This book argues that corporations across the plastics value chain are fuelling the ecological crisis through the pursuit of unlimited plastics growth, and what is more, they are getting away with it. Since the dramatic rise of plastics production after the Second World War, petrochemical and plastics corporations have fought to expand and protect plastics markets through manufacturing demand, denying risk, and co-opting solutions. Over the years, they have faced existential threats to business, first in a number of toxic scandals linking plastics to cancer and other illnesses, and later in relation to marine plastic waste and the climate crisis. Often, industry leaders have resorted to blatant deception to deny toxic risks in their quest to retain market control. Another industry tactic has been to shift blame to individual consumers and to poor infrastructure in Southeast Asia and Africa. Recently, corporations have become more sophisticated in their sustainability strategies, for example through adopting the circular economy agenda, appearing to embrace green initiatives while pursuing unsustainable growth. They have also played one crisis off against the other, proclaiming plastics in wind turbine blades and electric vehicles as the solution to climate change. Their aim has been to deflect public attention from the key problem: plastics production.

While waste is the most obvious manifestation of plastic pollution, the root of the plastics problem is not waste but production. Even at the height of the storm of public outrage over marine plastic litter, amid all the single-use plastics bans and corporate-sponsored beach clean-ups, global demand for plastics was on the rise. The largest market for plastics is for packaging, accounting for approximately 40% of global end markets. The second largest market is for building and construction at 20%.[2] New plastics markets are also rapidly proliferating in green technologies. According to the International Energy Agency (IEA), plastics will be the biggest driver of oil demand in the energy transition, reaching close to half of global oil demand by 2050.[3] Yet the increasing demand for plastics cannot keep up with the insatiable corporate drive for petrochemical expansion.

The petrochemical industry makes plastics from raw material 'feedstocks', which are derived from fossil fuels and other hydrocarbons through a process known as 'cracking', applying heat and pressure to break down heavy hydrocarbons into lighter molecules. Petrochemical expansion relies on (1) access to cheap and abundant 'virgin' (fossil fuel-based) feedstocks; and (2) continual growth in new plastics markets to absorb expanding production. The petrochemical industry is a cyclical industry, with boom-and-bust cycles of expansion and overcapacity.[4] In the decade leading up to the COVID-19 pandemic, there was a surge of petrochemical project investments around the world, linked to a range of factors including the availability of cheap liquefied natural gas (LNG) from fracking in the United States, the drop in oil prices in 2014, diversification into plastics from oil-producing countries (anticipating the energy transition), and strong GDP growth in China.[5] By the end of 2019, the petrochemical industry was heading into a downcycle. However, the COVID-19 pandemic delayed the predicted crisis of overcapacity.[6] The price of crude oil hit historic lows, new petrochemical projects stalled, and recycled plastic feedstocks became more expensive. Meanwhile, corporations used the health crisis to reverse single-use plastic bans and to roll back sustainability commitments. Demand for single-use plastics in packaging and personal protective equipment rocketed, offsetting short-term losses in other plastics markets, such as automotive products and appliances.[7] 'Looking forward, we're looking at fat margins,' a US industry executive commented in 2021. 'Not just in North America but around the world.'[8]

What can we do to stop the escalating plastics crisis? Despite the global momentum to address plastic pollution, policymakers have failed to challenge the capitalist imperative for unlimited plastics growth. We need to tackle this challenge head on. As a first step, let's take a closer look at the plastic facts.

The Plastic Facts

Within just a few years, the media landscape has become filled with facts about plastic. In December 2018, the fact that '9% of all plastic ever made has been recycled' was named the 'statistic of the year' by the British Royal Statistical Society.[9] Between 1950 and 2015, 8.3 billion metric tonnes of plastic were produced globally, 6.5 billion metric tonnes of which became plastic waste. Of that waste, 79% went to landfill or was leaked into the environment, 12% was incinerated, and 9% was recycled. Half of all plastic ever manufactured has been made since 2000.[10] The cumulative total of plastics production is expected to increase to the staggering amount of 34 billion metric tonnes by 2050, by which point plastic is predicted to outweigh fish in the oceans.[11] It is almost impossible to grasp these numbers, even with handy infographics about how many times around the earth we could line up all the plastic bags and bottles.

All plastics are polymers, meaning 'many parts' in Greek, made up of long chains of molecules with repeated units. Plastic polymer chains are composed of strong carbon bonds that can be combined with chemical additives to make just about anything. Petrochemicals derived from fossil fuels are used to make 99% of plastics,[12] and plastics markets account for 80% of petrochemical production.[13] Five main polymers make up 90% of all single-use plastics: polypropylene (PP); high-density polyethylene (HDPE); low-density polyethylene (LDPE); linear low-density polyethylene (LLDPE); and polyethylene terephthalate (PET).[14] The material qualities that make plastics so useful also make them flawed: everlasting, hydrocarbon-dependent, and easily fused with other substances. Instead of breaking down on a molecular level, plastics fragment into tiny pieces and persist in the environment. Our bodies and ecosystems are filled with petrochemicals and microplastics. Every stage of the plastics lifecycle, from extraction to refining to consumption and waste, poses significant risks to human health.[15] Plastics production releases toxic substances that are linked to cancer, neurological damage, and reproductive and developmental problems.[16] Toxic plastic pollution disproportionately impacts low-income and minority ethnic communities around the world.[17] Millions of animals are killed by plastics every year, primarily through starvation and entanglement.[18] The global environmental, health, and economic costs of plastic pollution are incalculable.

The list of facts goes on, all available with the tap of a finger on the Web. Unlike with global heating, there are no deniers of the plastics crisis. It is too tangible and traceable. Big brands Coca-Cola, PepsiCo, and Nestlé have been singled out by 'Break Free From Plastic' activists as the world's worst plastic polluters, based on an annual audit of hundreds of thousands of plastic items collected by volunteers.[19] Further upstream along the plastics value chain, a report by the Minderloo Foundation revealed that twenty major plastics producers (led by ExxonMobil, Dow, and Sinopec) accounted for more than half of all single-use plastic waste generated globally in 2019, and 100 accounted for more than 90%.[20] Instead of deniers, there are detractors: people who dismiss the plastics crisis as a distraction from the climate crisis, or who insist that it is eminently solvable through improving recycling and waste management systems.

Many plastic facts are widely accepted, while some are more contested. Researchers have pointed out that predictions of how many fish or plastics will be in the sea in the future, for example, are speculative and uncertain.[21] The petrochemical and plastics industries have taken advantage of public uncertainty about plastic facts to repeatedly cast doubt on scientific evidence about plastic toxicity in order to protect their markets.[22] They also claim that plastic packaging is more environmentally friendly than alternative materials, relying on assumptions about single-use packaging markets and consumer behaviour.[23] Other plastic facts are open to selective interpretation, such as the finding in 2018 that 90% of plastic waste in the ocean comes from just ten rivers, eight in Asia and two in Africa.[24] This led industry representatives to say: 'We know where the source of the problem is,' pointing to inadequate waste management infrastructure in these regions.[25] However, their framing occludes another fact: the highly unequal global trade in contaminated plastic waste. The largest exporters of plastic waste are the United States, Germany, and Japan. Since China announced a ban on plastic waste imports in 2017, global waste exports have been redirected to countries in Southeast Asia, which have struggled to cope with the inundation.[26] Several of these countries have returned contaminated shipments, and Thailand and Vietnam have announced plans to ban all plastic imports, but the traffic continues.[27] The global plastic waste trade is the latest frontier of 'waste colonialism', a term that politicians and activists have used to describe the unjust international trade in hazardous waste.[28]

After a deluge of depressing facts, the majority of books, films, and reports about the plastics crisis reach the same wilfully hopeful conclusion: that you can make a difference, by reducing your consumption of single-use plastics, recycling and reusing, and, if you're really keen, going on beach clean-ups and raising community awareness. Some anti-plastic campaigners have taken this mission to heart, writing detailed guidelines about how to live plastic-free within plastic-filled societies.[29] Other activists have taken aim at corporations. For example, the environmental NGO Greenpeace, the Break Free From Plastic movement, and the Changing Markets Foundation (which works in partnership with NGOs) have added plastic pollution to their long list of fossil fuel company sins and highlighted the 'false solutions' and 'paper promises' promoted by industry.[30] However, these claims tend to be dismissed by policy-makers and the public as ideological, following a predictable script of naming and shaming the 'top polluters'. This book makes a different kind of intervention. Rather than laying bare the contours of the crisis or lambasting the top polluters, the book asks: how did we get to this point, and what can we do about it? To begin with, where did the drive to make so much plastic come from?

Origin Stories

'I'm glad we have the Tupperware lady with us,' our instructor said to a room of twenty-five participants, mostly male, at a workshop on petrochemical markets in London.[31] The instructor was a former petrochemical manager with decades of experience in the industry, and his material was showing signs of ageing. He fetched some tatty-looking plastic containers from his satchel and laid them out on the corporate boardroom-style table, before launching into a discussion of polyethylene. 'Tupperware was the first commercial product from polyethylene, and the beginning of home-selling,' he began. Most of his plastic origin stories started with some kind of anecdote. Another one was about men using epoxy resins to fix their wives' broken teacups: 'Guys, this might work at home, but not in industry.' The 'Tupperware lady' and I made eye contact after this comment, and we shook our heads together.

The plastics industry is used to 'tired old jokes about plastic', as the industry's trade magazine referred in 1986 to the famous line from the 1968 film *The Graduate*: 'I just want to say one word to you ... just one word ... plastics. There's a great future in plastics.'[32] Today, plastics still carry associations with stereotypical images of post-war American life. Other old quotes have resurfaced from this period, acquiring ironic status with the benefit of hindsight. For example, there is the brazen remark from Lloyd Stouffer, the editor of *Modern Packaging Magazine*, that the 'future of the industry is in the trash can'.[33] This quote is from a speech that Stouffer gave to a plastics industry conference in 1956, where he argued that industry needed to switch from making reusable plastics to making single-use plastics, in order to increase their profits. It echoes the theme of the 1955 photo in *Life Magazine* captioned 'Throwaway Living', which has done rounds on social media, of a family celebrating amidst a swirling array of disposable household products, which promise to cut down on household chores.

One of the most prescient quotes circulating about plastic is by the French cultural theorist Roland Barthes, from his 1957 book *Mythologies* (translated into English in 1972). Barthes observed that 'more than a substance, plastic is the very idea of its infinite transformation', and reached an ominous conclusion: 'The hierarchy of substances is abolished: a single one replaces them all: the whole world can be plasticized, and even life itself since, we are told, they are beginning to make plastic aortas.'[34] This sounds like both a self-fulfilling prophecy and a dare. Indeed, industry realized the tantalising prospects of playing God with nature, and predictably ignored the Faustian implications. As a plastics executive exclaimed towards the end of the Second World War: '[V]irtually nothing was made from plastic and anything could be.'[35]

It's difficult to imagine the world before it became plasticized. The proliferation of plastics around the planet has been exponential, from the first plastics of the nineteenth century, to 2 million metric tonnes of plastics produced annually in 1950, to 368 million tonnes of annual plastics production in 2019.[36] Most histories of plastic begin with the invention of Parkesine in the mid-nineteenth century, a semi-synthetic plastic derived from cellulose that was used as a cheap substitute for ivory and tortoiseshell accessories.[37] According to environmental sociologist Rebecca Altman, a less-known story about celluloid is the fact that it 'accelerated the demand for camphor, a tree product used as a solvent and plasticizer', due to the rapid expansion of the celluloid market in the late nineteenth century for use in photographic and cinematic film.[38] Altman contends that the early history of bioplastics (plastics made from trees and plants) anticipated many of the environmental health and labour injustices that followed. For example, the extraction of tree resins, gums, and latex for rubber and celluloid production led to the violent displacement of Indigenous communities, deforestation, environmental destruction, and workplace hazards. The expression 'to be gassed' originated in nineteenth-century vulcanized rubber factories, where low-wage workers suffered from a range of neurological problems due to toxic exposures.[39] Viscose rayon, or 'fake silk', a fabric derived from cellulose, was also deadly to workers, leading to 'acute insanity in those it poisoned'.[40]

We touched on the early history of rubber at the workshop on petrochemical markets, as part of the C4 (four carbon bonds) butadiene value chain. Our instructor showed us a slide about the first rubber boom from 1879 to 1912, casually observing that 'natural rubber was Indigenous to Brazil, but all of the rubber trees in Brazil were killed off'.[41] Then he described how the British explorer Henry Wickham 'borrowed' 70,000 rubber seeds from Brazil, brought them to Kew Gardens in London, and set up plantations in Sri Lanka and Malaysia. However, the violence of this colonial history was only implied, as a taken-for-granted backdrop to the key story behind all plastic origin stories: chemical innovation, exemplified by the scientific achievement of duplicating nature in synthetic form.

The first fully synthetic plastic, Bakelite, was produced in 1907, a thermoset plastic that was hard and strong, but could not be remelted or remoulded. During the polymer science revolution of the 1920s and 1930s in Western Europe and the United States, a vast array of thermoplastics (mouldable at high temperatures) were synthesized for commercial use: polyvinyl chloride (PVC) in 1926; polystyrene in 1930; polyethylene in 1933; nylon in 1935; and polytetrafluoroethylene (later known as Teflon) in 1938. Historians of science and business typically focus on the key inventors and company rivalries during this period of intensive scientific innovation, with the interwar period as a backdrop.[42] It was the advent of the Second World War, though, that catapulted plastics onto the world stage of mass consumption.

The Second World War brought unprecedented demands for synthetic rubber, high-octane gasoline (using polymerized chemical additives), parachutes, aircraft components, bazooka barrels, mortar fuses, helmet liners, radar insulation, and a wide range of other military plastics uses.[43] Plastics were even crucial for the atom bomb: fluorocarbon plastics (related to polytetrafluoroethylene) were used to contain the volatile gases.[44] The war sparked the rapid growth of the petrochemical industry, which began using the by-products of oil (rather than coal) to create plastic resins, the building blocks of plastic products. Massive petrochemical plants sprang up next to oil refineries in the United States and Europe. Anticipating the glut of petrochemical capacity after the war, major chemical companies began to search for new uses for petrochemical products. DuPont started designing prototypes of plastic houseware products that could be marketed to consumers, with the advertising slogan 'Better Things for Better Living ... through Chemistry'.[45]

The petrochemical and plastics industries, like many modern capitalist industries, grew out of war. Yet there is an even darker side to this origin story. In the interwar period, the German chemical conglomerate IG Farben, one of the main players in the polymer science revolution, led an international cartel of corporations that restricted global trade in synthetic oil and rubber. During the Second World War, IG Farben operated a concentration camp using slave labour on one of its industrial sites, conducted medical experiments on prisoners, and supplied the toxic gas Zyklon B to the concentration camps.[46] In 1941, the United States conducted an antitrust investigation into Standard Oil (now Exxon) and its six subsidiaries for conspiring with IG Farben to restrict trade, indicting three corporate leaders, who resigned.[47] Twenty-three of IG Farben's directors were tried by the US Military Tribunal sitting at Nuremberg between 1947 and 1949 for war crimes and crimes against humanity, thirteen of whom were convicted. This was a hallmark international case for holding business leaders responsible for corporate crimes.[48]

In the aftermath of the Second World War, the petrochemical cartels dissolved. In 1951, IG Farben was broken up into different companies, including BASF, Bayer, and Hoechst, which each gained their own legal identities. However, tacit cooperation continued between the leading American and European petrochemical companies.[49] This laid the historical foundations of industrial collaboration and collusion that continued in the toxic scandals of later years. The exponential growth of plastics in the post-war period was not an inevitable outcome of material innovation, as it is often framed, but a legacy of war.

Unlimited Plastics

The European plastics industry celebrated '100 Years of Plastics' in December 2020 with the launch of a website about how plastics make life better and more sustainable. The tagline: 'Unlimited Possibilities for the Future'.[50] The hallmark achievement in 1920 was the publication of a ground-breaking research article by the German scientist and Nobel Prize winner Hermann Staudinger, which formed the basis for modern polymer science. A collaboration between the Macromolecular Chemistry Division of the Association of German Chemists and Plastics Europe Deutschland (the German branch of the Plastics Europe industry association), the website features monthly articles that showcase ways that plastics help society. The first article, 'Plastics During the Pandemic', singles out five plastics applications as making material contributions to COVID-19: protective clothing; plastics machinery (for making masks and other equipment); protective walls (transparent partition walls); medical sector materials; and the transport of vaccines (in insulated frozen boxes).[51] Notably absent from this list are plastic bags and disposable food and beverage containers, which the industry had so actively promoted as the 'sanitary choice' at the beginning of the pandemic.[52] Despite its centennial theme, the '100 Years of Plastic' website avoids any mention of the wartime origins of modern plastics. Instead of reflecting on the past, it speculates on the future, using the occasion to capture the celebratory mood of the plastics revival of the pandemic. The unlimited possibilities for the future of plastics, naturally, are all about perpetual growth.

The capitalist pursuit of unlimited growth is the key problem underlying the plastics crisis. It is not unique to the plastics industry, but rather the defining feature of all corporations within modern capitalism. Publicly traded corporations are legally obliged to act in the 'best interests' of shareholders, which most people interpret to mean maximizing profits and growth. However, as anti-trust lawyer Michelle Meagher argues, the powerful norm of shareholder value exists only weakly in law and is unenforceable. In other words, according to Meagher: 'Shareholder value is not the law – or it does not have to be, if we collectively agree that it is not.'[53] Meagher notes that when corporations were first created in England in the seventeenth century to fund public projects, 'the norm of accountability was not limited liability but actually *unlimited* liability', as their principal obligation was to fulfil their public purpose. Of course, Meagher reminds us, the 'public' purpose that these early corporations served was tied to the colonial ambitions of the British Empire, but her point is that the norms governing corporations can change. The limited liability of the modern corporation, in her view, 'removes responsibility and accountability'.[54]

Recently, business leaders have attempted to cast the corporation's shareholder purpose in a new light. In April 2019, the Business Roundtable of more than 200 of the world's top CEOs proclaimed that the new purpose of publicly traded corporations would be to serve the interests not only of shareholders but also of workers, communities, and the environment.[55] This exemplifies what law professor Joel Bakan describes as the 'new' corporation of the twenty-first century: 'doing well by doing good', or 'making money through social and environmental values rather than in spite of them'.[56] The problem, Bakan argues, is that the legal structure of corporations – enforced by the profit-seeking imperative of capitalism – requires that they will always prioritize doing well over doing good. Furthermore, as the political scientist Peter Dauvergne observes, the business case for corporate sustainability is not just about deflecting criticism; it is also about gaining corporate power over regulations.[57]

Corporations Across the Plastics Value Chain

Often, critics of the plastics industry lump all plastics corporations together, using the term 'Big Plastic' to apply equally to oil, packaging, consumer goods, and beverage companies.[58] For example, in September 2020, the Changing Markets Foundation published the report *Talking Trash: The Corporate Playbook of False Solutions*, which accused 'Big Plastic' of 'two-faced hypocrisy' for claiming to be committed to solutions to the plastics crisis, while obstructing and undermining legislative solutions to it.[59] Although there are many similarities and collaborations between Big Plastic companies, however, there are also important differences. Corporations across the plastics value chain span a wide range of interconnected industries, from fossil fuels (oil, gas, and coal) and biofuels (sugar and biomass), to petrochemicals (transforming hydrocarbons into plastic resins), plastics converters (converting plastic resins into packaging and other end uses), plastic end markets (e.g., food and beverage companies and other 'fast-moving consumer goods' or FMCG companies), and waste management and recycling.

One of the main differences between these industry segments is their relative size and power. Until recently, the majority of public attention has focused on the top plastics polluters at the downstream end of the sector, due to the high visibility of plastic packaging waste. In particular, many NGOs and activists have singled out big brands in the consumer goods and beverage industries (e.g., Procter & Gamble, Unilever, Coca-Cola, and Nestlé), which rely heavily on single-use plastic packaging. Increasingly, however, researchers and policymakers have shifted their attention upstream to the plastics producers in the petrochemical industry, with concerns about the industry's anti-competitive practices, lack of transparency, toxic pollution, and continuing reliance on fossil fuels.[60] A relatively small number of very large firms dominate the market through technological advantage and access to cheap feedstocks, creating strong barriers to entry with economies of scale and scope.[61] The top plastics producers by annual turnover are vertically integrated oil and gas companies (e.g., ExxonMobil, Saudi Aramco, Chevron Philips) and multinational chemical companies (e.g., BASF, Dow, DuPont, INEOS), which operate thousands of production sites worldwide, clustered in massive petrochemical complexes next to oil refineries, pipelines, and ports. They also have the strongest voices within plastics industry trade associations such as the World Plastics Council, the Plastics Industry Association, Plastics Europe, the European Petrochemical Association, and the American Chemistry Council.

In the middle of the plastics value chain, sandwiched between the consumer goods giants and the plastics producers, is the less-visible plastics converter sector. The majority of the plastics industry, in terms of both the number of businesses and the number of employees, is concentrated in the plastics converter sector.[62] The plastics converters include a handful of global packaging companies (e.g., Novolex, Amcor, Berry Global), which rival the major petrochemical companies and big brands in terms of annual profits, but the sector as a whole is made up of primarily small and medium-sized enterprises. Then there is the recycling and waste management sector at the post-consumer end of the plastics value chain, which is also dominated by a few major players (e.g., Veolia Environmental, Republic Services). Over the past few years, several petrochemical corporations have partnered with recycling and waste management firms in response to the plastics crisis and circular economy policies.

Geopolitical differences are also significant. Up until the end of the twentieth century, the petrochemical industry was dominated by many of the same powerful oil and chemical companies that were 'first movers' in the early development of the industry in the United States, Western Europe, and Japan.[63] While some of these corporations have remained top global players, notably ExxonMobil, BASF, and Dow, other corporations have entered the top ten list of global chemical companies, including Sinopec (China), SABIC (Saudi Arabia), Formosa Plastics (Taiwan), and INEOS (UK).[64] There has been a dramatic growth in state-owned corporations in Asia, the Middle East, and South America, which now account for 30% of plastics producers worldwide.[65] In the first two decades of the twenty-first century, China rose to become the top plastics producer and consumer in the world, overtaking the United States and Europe. During this period, other countries in Asia also became major zones for plastics production and consumption. Meanwhile, petrochemical investments in the United States, and to some extent in Europe, have been bolstered by the availability of cheap LNG feedstocks from the US shale gas revolution. The private petrochemical giant INEOS, owned by UK billionaire Jim Ratcliffe, has profited immensely from shale gas. Over the next decade, China's growth is set to account for 28% of global petrochemical capacity additions, followed by India at 17% and Iran at 10%.[66] This predicted expansion in plastics production is based on the industry's success at promoting global demand for plastic products, which is expected to continue irrespective of policies to address plastic pollution.[67]

Each industry segment has its own market position and set of interests within the plastics value chain. For example, the bioplastics industry (which uses bio-based feedstocks such as sugar and corn flour to make plastics) favours the substitution of virgin feedstocks with renewable resources, as contrasted with the mainstream plastics industry, but both oppose single-use plastics bans.[68] Furthermore, corporations across the plastics value chain are heterogeneous, both within and across industry segments, with different cultures, traditions, and ambitions. Many state-owned enterprises, while competing in global capital markets, are driven by national and regional interests, such as China's goal of energy self-sufficiency and the quest for diversification in oil-producing countries. Some corporations have been leaders in their voluntary sustainability commitments, at least in relative terms, for example through disclosing their plastic packaging footprints, while others have been laggards.

When it comes to the business of limits, though, corporations across the global plastics value chain do have some common interests. First, they each benefit from the problem of societal dependence. Unlimited plastics growth is inherently destructive and unsustainable, but modern societies have become too dependent on plastics to phase them out easily. Plastics are cheap, durable, and incredibly versatile, enmeshed in almost every aspect of modern life, from buildings to agriculture, healthcare, transport, clothing, and electronic devices. Second, in material terms, plastics represent seemingly unlimited possibilities for growth into new uses and markets, allowing corporations to constantly create the conditions for future plastics dependence. Third, given their reliance on fossil fuels, most corporations across the plastics value chain have vested interests in maintaining 'business as usual', enabled by powerful financial actors including investors, banks, insurance companies, and governments. Despite international regulations to address plastic pollution and the climate crisis, petrochemical and plastics companies have received extensive government subsidies, keeping artificially low costs of virgin feedstocks.[69] On an existential level, corporations are wilfully ignorant about the problem of unlimited plastics growth, which is not only delusional but also self-destructive. Plastics growth will inevitably reach limits, imposed by the end of fossil fuels and biofuels, or by the mass extinctions that come with toxic pollution, climate disruptions, and biodiversity loss – whichever comes first. This means that unless there are serious political interventions, by the time plastics reach material limits, it will be too late.

For decades, corporations across the plastics value chain have developed powerful tools for protecting their interests through a combination of expertise and wilful ignorance. On the one hand, the leading corporations maintain market dominance through advanced scientific, technological, and economic expertise, from cutting-edge polymer science and chemical engineering to detailed knowledge of international and national laws, geopolitical and environmental risks, and market forecasts. They use their multiscalar expertise to their economic advantage, anticipating regulations, denying toxic hazards, and promoting risky new technologies.[70] On the other hand, corporations are wilfully ignorant about their responsibility for social and environmental harms. Wilful ignorance is where people recognize that they are part of the problem but avoid confronting it, often through seeking forms of justification. We all do this, but as the sociologists Linsey McGoey and Hannah Jones argue, sometimes the act of looking away is strategic, to avoid legal liability, or violent, whether intentional or not.[71] Through their wilful ignorance, corporations across the value chain avoid taking responsibility for environment injustice: the disproportionate exposure of communities of colour and poor communities to toxic pollution and waste.[72]

This book focuses on corporations within powerful industries, rather than on the individuals who run them per se. Joel Bakan writes that it is crucial 'to stay focused on the corporation *as an institution*, on how its legal structure compels the people who run companies to do what they do. ... Some may personally believe in the corporate values that frame their work, while others may not.'[73] I agree that the people who run corporations are often guided by business imperatives to put the interests of profit over the interests of the public, regardless of their personal values. However, the narrative of 'bad' corporations versus 'good' individuals misses another important issue: the extent to which destructive worldviews and wilful ignorance have been normalized to the point of appearing benign. Even the most well-intentioned corporative executives find ways of passing the blame and reframing their own motivations as irreproachable. In *The Value of Everything*, economist Mariana Mazzucato makes a critical intervention into this problem, arguing that policymakers have lost the ability to distinguish between value creation and value destruction, due to a false narrative about corporate wealth creators, risk taking, and entrepreneurship which has become entrenched within political and public discourse. The consequence is that 'those who claim to be wealth creators have monopolized the attention of governments with the now well-worn mantra of: give us less tax, less regulation, less state and more market', which has 'made it easier for some to call themselves value creators and in the process extract value'.[74] This is what needs to change.

Confronting Crisis

The adage 'never let a good crisis go to waste' has been widely attributed to Winston Churchill, who is said to have made this comment during the Yalta Conference with Stalin and Roosevelt near the end of the Second World War.[75] During the financial crisis of 2008, Rahm Emanuel, Obama's Chief of Staff, also used this expression, and it has since become popular among business and political leaders.[76] In February 2020, Bernard Looney, the newly appointed CEO of British Petroleum (BP), quoted the 'great Winston Churchill phrase' in his keynote address at International

Petroleum (IP) Week in London, talking about the
climate crisis 'as an opportunity for the industry to
significantly reshape how it works'.[77] Not surprisingly,
the phrase has also invited more critical interpretations.
In *Never Let a Serious Crisis Go to Waste*, historian
Philip Mirowski argues that neoliberals survived the
2008 Great Recession by using the opportunity of
the crisis to consolidate power.[78] Naomi Klein makes
a related argument in *The Shock Doctrine*, detailing
how political and economic elites have exploited the
upheavals of national disasters to push forward controversial neoliberal free market policies.[79]

The idea that capitalism is well equipped to accom-
modate crisis is very familiar among social scientists.
It is such a common trope that many scholars avoid
the term 'crisis' altogether. For example, the anthro-
pologist Joe Masco argues that '"crisis" has become a
counterrevolutionary idiom in the twenty-first century,
a means of stabilizing an existing condition rather than
minimizing forms of violence across militarism, economy,
and the environment'.[80] In *Pollution Is Colonialism*,
interdisciplinary plastic pollution scholar Max Liboiron
characterizes 'crisis as a relational model that puts certain
things beyond dispute in the imperative to act at all
costs'.[81] In a similar vein, environmental scholar-activists
Matt Hern and Am Johal caution that '[c]risis invokes
an emergency where debate is suspended, reflection
limited, and objections marginalized. The implications of
invoking a climate crisis are all too vivid: it is into this
breach where hegemonic states and capital step so easily
and so reassuringly.'[82] Other scholars suggest that the
plastic waste crisis, in particular, suffers from inaction
due to the 'environmental crisis industry', which 'perpet-
uates stasis in the face of environmental catastrophe'.[83]

Indeed, political and economic elites are constantly
poised to seize the opportunities of crisis to gain power
and wealth. But why should we relinquish talk of crisis

to elites? I am not convinced that the imperative to act on the ecological crisis requires suspending debate or limiting reflection. On the contrary, it requires deeper debate and reflection, even if the timescales are tight.

I am also worried about a related trend: the normalization of crisis. In May 2019, the *Guardian* wrote that they were changing their house style for referring to the climate: 'Instead of "climate change" the preferred terms are "climate emergency, crisis or breakdown" and "global heating" is favoured over "global warming".'[84] This was part of a broader shift towards perpetual talk of crisis in the media and public culture. However, the way that the media both sensationalizes and normalizes crisis has the danger of desensitizing us, robbing us of the power to even elicit a response. Hence there is crisis fatigue, a state of exhaustion, which has deepened through the waves of the pandemic. It is both literal, for the great number of people who have struggled every day to cope and to survive, and psychological, for those who have observed the unfolding disasters from a distance, full of feelings of anxiety and powerlessness.

Yet the reality, injustice, and urgency of crisis cannot be avoided. We must tackle the source of the plastics crisis in order to mitigate the worst impacts of the ecological catastrophe. The plastics crisis, and public responses to it, did not simply arrive in the world over the last few years. Since the 1970s, a number of social and environmental movements have tried to limit harmful plastics production and pollution. Global media attention to the plastics crisis has raised levels of anti-plastic activism around the world. Some of this momentum has continued through the pandemic, with calls for a new global treaty on plastic pollution.[85] Yet in spite of the surge of legislation and activism, the plastics crisis is only getting worse. The rate of plastics growth is exponential, and it appears to be unstoppable. The obstacle is not one of inaction, but one of entanglement.

For all of the toxicity and pollution associated with plastic, it is difficult to imagine living without it. Plastic is essential to modern life, from computers to washing machines to food supplies and medical equipment. COVID-19 has been an important reminder of this fact. Yet most plastic is not essential. Nor does it have to be. To disentangle ourselves from toxic and wasteful plastics, we need to retrace the steps of our entanglement, starting with the corporations.

This book examines how corporations across the plastics value chain have fought to secure and grow toxic, wasteful, and carbon-intensive processes and markets despite a series of crises: plastic toxicity (chapter 2), marine plastic waste (chapter 3), the climate emergency (chapter 4), the COVID-19 pandemic (chapter 5), and the cumulative plastics crisis (chapter 6). Drawing on publicly available corporate materials, observations at industry events, and interviews with industry representatives,[86] in addition to a range of scholarly, media, NGO, and policy sources, the book focuses on the dominant corporate players and alliances that have mobilized in each case, which differ depending on which markets have been threatened. For example, the noxious petrochemical industry has covered up plastics toxicity, the leading plastics bag producers have actively opposed plastic bag bans, oil majors have funded climate change denial, and multinational beverage brands have opposed bottle deposit schemes. On a systemic level, the relentless corporate drive to expand petrochemical production and to seek out new plastics markets has been underpinned by a reliance on shifting the toxic burdens of pollution and waste disposal onto the most vulnerable populations. Rather than seeing crisis as a means for elites to stabilize the status quo, this book argues that we need to confront the corporate roots of the crisis to bring about systemic change.

2

Manufacturing Toxic Wants and Needs

Over the past few years, the paradox of plastic as both a miracle and a menace for society has become a platitude. There are countless stories in the media and popular culture about our fraught relationship with plastic, focusing on our addiction and dependence.[1] However, this way of framing the problem actually serves to perpetuate it. Plastics are plural. There are tens of thousands of plastics, each with different physical properties, including not only flexibility or durability, but also toxicity. By lumping plastics together into a singular entity with both beneficial and harmful features, the double-sided narrative assumes that the two sides can never be separated. By blaming us all for our dependence on plastic, questions of corporate responsibility and unequal toxic risks are avoided. Ultimately, the paradox of plastic conveys a sense of inescapability that industry can tap into.

'Let's talk realistically about plastic' is the title of a campaign launched in October 2020 by the Danish Plastics Federation, featuring short videos with plastic reality-check messages: 'Without plastic

... cars would use more fuel'; 'No plastic ... no bike helmet.' The punchline: 'Frankly, we need plastic where it makes sense. But a world without ... creates more problems than it solves.'[2] The US-based Plastics Industry Association regularly tweets and blogs similar messages. For example, one blog post decried the public's 'knee-jerk reaction' of proposing plastic bans and substitutions to deal with plastic litter as 'overly simplistic', 'outlandish', and 'impractical ... like when a child proposes that the solution to global warming is eliminating cars'.[3]

While this line of argument is 'overly simplistic' itself, the industry is right in some ways. Plastic cannot be separated neatly into different piles of societal value: of essential versus wasteful, or desirable versus toxic. Many plastics are indeed essential for health and safety, transport, and connectivity, yet are also toxic and wasteful. There are no easy solutions to such a complex problem. However, we can stop the plastics crisis from spiralling even further out of control. Many plastic products can and should be banned or substituted to protect health, the environment, and the climate. Policymakers, researchers, and activists have rightly focused on the need to eliminate or substitute the production of toxic plastic products (to protect health), single-use plastics (to stop the plastic waste crisis), and virgin (fossil fuel-based) plastics (to address the climate crisis). There are many barriers and dilemmas involved in such proposals, as the chapters in this book will discuss, but reducing harmful plastics production is not an unrealistic goal. On the contrary, it is both possible and necessary. An important start is to interrogate corporate half-truths as well as untruths.

The industry's 'realistic versus impractical' narrative is a pragmatic twist on a related narrative that has long been popular with industry: 'reality versus fiction', used to make truth claims about the benefits and non-toxicity of plastics. Since the beginning of the plastic age, industry has tirelessly promoted the essential and desirable characteristics of plastic products, while denying their harmful effects. The discovery of synthetic plastics over a century ago was seen as miraculous, saving animals by replacing ivory and tortoiseshell, and natural resources by replacing wood, silk, and glass.[4] More importantly for a capitalist system, plastics were cheap. After the Second World War, new plastic household products entered the market, fostering the growth of mass consumer society. Steadfastly, industry extended its reach into other markets, to building materials, shopping bags, medical equipment, toys, electronics, water bottles, and food packaging. People were sold not only plastics but also the idea of disposability.

Yet the public has never been fully sold on plastics. From the start, labour, consumer, and environmental groups have questioned the production and use of plastics. In fact, the petrochemical and plastics industries have often been accused of using the playbook from Big Tobacco by manufacturing doubt and uncertainty about the hazards of their products.[5] I wish that I could say that these accusations are exaggerated, or oversimplify a more complicated situation, but if anything, they are understated. In the 1960s and early 1970s, the American and European petrochemical industries conspired to conceal scientific links between vinyl chloride, cancer, and other illnesses, in order to protect their markets.[6] The news about vinyl chloride and cancer broke in 1974, leading to public alarm and swift regulations, but it took decades for researchers and lawyers to expose the corporate lies and cover-ups. Meanwhile, industry learned how to anticipate regulations, refining its 'deceit and denial' tactics in later controversies over carcinogenic and hormone-disrupting plastics.

Beyond high-stakes battles over truth, corporations often ignore issues of toxicity altogether, especially given that the burden of proof for harm rests on communities, not corporations. In spite of decades of environmental justice struggles around the world, toxic hazards from plastics remain disproportionately located in minority, low-income, and working-class communities. In Canada, my home country, the Indigenous Aamjiwanaang First Nation is located next to a number of toxic polluting petrochemical plants in 'Chemical Valley' in Sarnia, Ontario, and local residents have reported a number of illnesses.[7] This parallels the infamous case of 'Cancer Alley' in Louisiana, an 85-mile stretch of former plantation land along the Mississippi River with a high concentration of petrochemical facilities and oil refineries situated in close proximity to rural Black residential communities.[8] Indeed, around the world there are hundreds of 'cancer villages' and cancer clusters related to plastics production, incineration, and disposal.[9] Some corporations have been held to account for negligent toxic waste, and air quality regulations have been introduced in many places, but most companies have continued with business as usual. Despite the risks and negative social and environmental impacts, corporations across the plastics value chain will deploy whatever tactics they can in order to create, protect, and expand plastics markets.

Overcoming Limits

At the inaugural meeting of the European Petrochemical Association in 1967 in Deauville, France, Monsanto executive Eric Yates declared in his keynote address:

> From its basic origin as a satellite of the petroleum, coal and chemical industry, petrochemicals has emerged as

an industry of its own. Petrochemicals, as an industry, is now only in its second decade. Its growth has been phenomenal in the 1960s and the forecasts for the future are such that we can still look at the industry as an infant.

Yates carried on with the theme of exponential growth, noting that the problems arising from growth of such magnitude were now becoming apparent. He was vague about the nature of these problems, referring obliquely to difficulties of communication, recognition, and representation within and beyond the industry. He suggested that the only way to find solutions was through establishing a 'truly petrochemical industry organization', beyond the industry's roots in the US National Petroleum Refiners Association (NPRA).[10] The industry needed to organize to ensure that its growth would continue.

Since the start of the post-war proliferation of plastics, the key challenge for industry has been about overcoming the limits to plastics growth. The first limit that industry faced was the lack of demand for the newly synthesized polymers. In the immediate post-war period, petrochemical and plastics companies focused their efforts on inventing a wide range of new uses for plastics and marketing them to consumers.[11] The second limit was the breakdown in public trust. The publication of Rachel Carson's *Silent Spring* in 1962, the vinyl chloride scandals of the 1970s, and the toxic chemical disasters in Seveso (Italy) in 1973, Love Canal (United States) in 1978, and Bhopal (India) in 1984 all drew widespread public attention to the environmental and health dangers of the petrochemical industry.[12] In response to these concerns, industry leaders developed coordinated strategies to deflect criticisms, defend their markets, and regain public trust. The third limit was cyclical crisis: the chronic tendency towards overproduction and overcapacity, which led to waves of industry consolidation over the years, through mergers and joint ventures, linked to intense competition and the shifting geopolitics of oil and gas.[13]

From the vantage point of the present moment, it may seem that the petrochemical and plastics industries have succeeded in their goal of overcoming the limits to growth. But the problem is that there are no limits when it comes to the capitalist logic of perpetual economic growth.[14] There will always be more possible uses and markets, more investments to be made, and more stormy business cycles to ride out. The influential biologist and environmentalist Barry Commoner captured this destructive logic very well in an essay in 2001 on the threat of the petrochemical industry to planetary life:

> Today's chemical industry executive might be excused for regarding his predecessor as the Sorcerer's Apprentice: able to create the industry, but unaware of its threats to health and the environment. Yet, it remains important to learn why the industry blundered into these troubles. One answer to this question is given by the research policy enunciated by the Hooker Chemical Company, a pioneer, now extinct, petrochemical company: 'Rather than manufacturing known products by a known method for a known market … the research department is now … free to develop any product that looks promising. If there is not a market for it, the sales development group seeks to create one.'[15]

Creating Markets

The key to creating demand for plastics has always been about material competition. 'Not a single solid market for plastics in existence today was eagerly waiting for these materials,' remarked the editor of the trade journal *Modern Plastics* in 1956. To gain markets after the Second World War, each new plastic product needed to overcome 'either fearsome competition from vested materials or inertia and misunderstandings in acceptance'.[16] In other words, people had to be convinced of the advantages of plastics. The most obvious advantages were cheapness and availability. However, many of the first plastic products broke easily, such as Mackintosh raincoats made from wartime PVC scrap, earning plastics a bad reputation for shoddiness. Moreover, people who had carefully saved, mended, and reused during the war were sceptical of disposable products and reluctant to throw them away.[17] There were some serious mishaps, too. The first consumer plastic bags in the 1950s resulted in the deaths of eight children by smothering.[18]

Throughout the 1960s and 1970s, plastic took on negative cultural connotations of falseness, insincerity, and superficiality. One industry expert blamed the 1977 film *Saturday Night Fever* for hampering plastics markets by embedding public perceptions of polyester as a low-class fabric.[19] Another major setback for plastics during this time was the growing environmental movement, spurred by the series of toxic chemical disasters around the world. The industry was no longer to be trusted to keep people safe.

Over time, though, in market after market, plastics won over. Industry ran aggressive marketing campaigns, from the cheery advertisements for disposable products in the 1950s to the multimillion-dollar 'Plastics Make It Possible' initiative launched in the 1990s. Polyester soon found new markets, with the rise of the PET soda bottle in the 1970s and 1980s, which displaced glass and revolutionized single-use packaging.[20] After a series of false starts, plastic shopping bags finally conquered their paper equivalents in US supermarkets in the 1980s. Each plastic story developed in a similar fashion, from initial introduction, to gradual acceptance, to near-total market domination and proliferation. Some plastics markets eventually stalled: the fad for Hula Hoops subsided, and foamed polystyrene food and beverage packaging sales plunged in the 1990s over toxicity concerns. But most markets took off and never stopped growing. In many cases, low-cost availability and convenience were the main selling points. Beyond cheap imitation, plastics also offered new possibilities in terms of performance, for example in shatterproof glass, heat-resistant building materials, and flexible medical tubing.

In *American Plastic*, historian Jeffrey Meikle argues that plastic only gained widespread public acceptance in the 1990s, as the first generation to have grown up with plastic came of age.[21] By then, plastics had become embedded in modern devices to such an extent that they were no longer even seen as plastic, but as part of the new information age. Industry had also invested heavily in public relations campaigns and recycling technologies to improve the image of plastics. However, further public concerns about plastics emerged in the 1990s over the health effects of toxic chemicals leaching from consumer products, concerns that still plague the industry today.

'The only market we can't reach is beer and wine,' boasted one industry representative at a workshop on petrochemical markets that I attended in Rotterdam early in 2018. 'The public just won't accept wine in plastic bottles. Except in aeroplanes.'[22] This was where I first made the connection between wasteful plastics markets and petrochemical growth. In our dizzying day-long tour through the major polymers and their myriad applications, I could see that the vast majority of end products were wasteful and non-essential. While there were many 'essential' plastic products in the mix, such as bicycle helmets, heart valves, and wind turbine blades, these represented only a fraction of end markets. Furthermore, the workshop, pitched at corporate managers from across the plastics value chain, revealed industry knowledge about toxicity concerns for a large number of products, both historically and in the present day. The wilful ignorance behind the marketing of wasteful and toxic products was plainly evident and disturbingly blasé.

Yet the battle to create new plastics markets is far from over. As I discuss in later chapters, material competition comes into play whenever new markets are created, such as green technologies. It becomes particularly fierce whenever substitutions are proposed.

Protecting Markets

Of all the problems with plastics, the gravest is their capacity to cause illness and death. Plastic toxicity posed the first existential threat to the industry, and it has remained the industry's most enduring yet deliberately sidelined risk. Major petrochemical corporations no longer publicly deny climate change, nor do they question the issue of plastic waste. They have developed other tactics to deflect these, namely co-opting the solutions and shifting the blame. But corporations do continue to deny the toxic health risks of plastics, despite overwhelming scientific evidence to the contrary.

Why, given all the focus on corporate social responsibility today, do they keep up the denial? For one thing, toxicity remains a fundamental threat to lucrative plastics markets. Substances with known health hazards tend to be either heavily regulated or banned outright. For another, it is relatively easy to cast doubt on scientific studies linking toxic exposures with chronic illnesses. As the epidemiologist David Michaels observes in *Doubt Is Their Product*, an exposé about the corporate abuses of science: 'By its nature, epidemiology is a sitting duck for uncertainty campaigns.' The scientific rules for establishing links between exposure and disease are far more likely to find a false negative, he says, than a false positive. That is why 'waiting for absolute proof is a recipe for failure: people will die.'[23]

Corporations also have time on their side. In the early post-war period, the toxic health effects of the newly synthesized plastics were largely unknown. On the assumption that plastics were considered safe until proven dangerous, industry built massive petrochemical plants and produced vast quantities of plastics for growing consumer markets. Thus, before any alarm bells sounded over safety concerns, extensive plastic infrastructures and supply chains had already become interwoven with everyday life.

Take blood bags, for example, which use di(2-ethylhexyl) phthalate (DEHP) as a plasticizer to soften PVC. Plasticized PVC blood bags were introduced in the 1960s to replace glass, on the presumption that PVC was chemically stable and non-toxic. DEHP even had the added benefit of prolonging shelf-life, acting as a preservative for red blood cells.[24] Like many other plastic products, PVC blood bags soon became ubiquitous, and plasticized PVC was rolled out across other medical applications, such as tubing. During a workshop on petrochemical markets – the one with the 'Tupperware lady' – our instructor brushed off toxicity concerns about phthalates by pointing to the blood bag: 'If it ain't broke, don't fix it. There have been no issues.'[25] Not surprisingly, however, there *have* been issues with DEHP in blood bags, which leaches out of PVC and has been linked to lowered male fertility, breast cancer, liver cancer, and other illnesses.[26] Since the 1990s, there have been a number of health campaigns around the world to get hospitals to stop using PVC, for example campaigns by the environmental organization Health Care Without Harm.[27] However, without marketable alternatives to PVC blood bags (lightweight, inexpensive, and with long shelf-lives), regulators have reasoned that for now the life-saving benefits outweigh the risks. 'By the way,' the instructor added. 'The new car smell we all like is from the plasticizer.'

The longer corporations can sustain denial and uncertainty, the more time they can buy to avoid regulations and bans. In the case of plastics, they got an early start. In *Deceit and Denial*, historians Gerald Markowitz and David Rosner unveil the astonishing paper trail of a decade-long conspiracy within industry to hide scientific evidence about the harmful health effects of the vinyl chloride monomer used to make PVC.[28] In the mid-1960s, industry leaders discovered that several workers in their vinyl chloride plants were afflicted by acro-osteolysis, a rare degenerative bone disease. Worried about the potential business implications, the industry quietly funded further scientific research into the possible health risks of vinyl chloride. It learned that vinyl chloride was linked not only to acro-osteolysis but also to a number of cancers, and that the health effects were evident at surprisingly low levels of exposure. When confronted about the issue, industry representatives blatantly lied to regulatory agencies.

In 1974, four workers at a vinyl chloride plant died from the same rare cancer, angiosarcoma. This was a smoking gun, epidemiologically speaking, and the plant managers were unable to stop the news from getting out. The result was highly unfavourable to industry: strict environmental regulations were imposed for workplace exposure limits; vinyl aerosol products were taken off the market; and industry's warnings of economic catastrophe proved wrong. It learned its lesson: don't leave a paper trail, and don't let regulators make sudden moves.

The vinyl chloride scandal has entered the annals of corporate infamy, in league with the 'merchants of doubt' of the oil and tobacco industries.[29] While petrochemical corporations have diversified their strategies for protecting markets over the years, they have never stopped using the old playbook. To this day, industry continues to defend many plastics that have been scientifically proven to be harmful to human health, including bisphenol A (BPA) and phthalates in plasticizers, both of which have been banned in certain applications, such as children's toys (in some countries), but are still widely used in other products. Industry associations from across the plastics value chain regularly produce industry-backed research to cast doubt on scientific evidence about plastic toxicity; lobby regulators to avoid market restrictions; and publicize their dismay at regulatory decisions that they claim are based on politics, not science. In the post-truth era, industry representatives often simply dismiss scientific reports about plastic toxicity as 'fake news', 'misleading', and 'biased'.

Having prolonged controversy about the toxic effects of plastics for decades, industry now claims that regulatory recommendations to restrict products are based on old studies and data, with the implication that they are no longer valid. For example, in 2018, the American Academy of Pediatrics (AAP) published a policy statement about the problem of harmful chemicals in food packaging, including BPA, which is associated with endocrine (hormone) disruption. The Plastics Association issued a response challenging the data:

> We've reviewed the AAP new policy statement, released this week, which isn't based on any newly-released studies or data. The AAP references studies that suggest associations between exposure to food packaging materials and toxicity, but these data fail to establish causation. Correlations are not causation. For example, the AAP links BPA to obesity among low-income and

minority children, without acknowledging other well-documented and plausible risk factors such as living in food deserts without access to fruits and vegetables.[30]

Industry never tires of making the 'correlation versus causation' case against epidemiological studies, or pointing to confounding factors, classic 'tricks of the trade' in sowing uncertainty.[31] In the throes of the public outcry over marine plastic waste in 2018, an industry executive warned corporate managers that there were 'real and growing threats to many plastic products ... based on a combination of facts and fiction, but fiction becomes reality if it is believed by the public'. Under 'facts', he acknowledged that plastic bags were a real litter problem which hurt wildlife and had very low levels of recycling. Under 'fiction', he put all the claims about the toxicity of consumer products that had been around since the 1990s, including PVC (due to phthalates), polycarbonate (due to BPA), and polystyrene foam (due to styrene, a known carcinogen).[32]

There are ongoing legal battles today over the toxic health effects of many chemicals, including perfluorooctanoic acid (PFOA) and other per- and polyfluoroalkyl substances (PFAS), known as 'forever chemicals', used for decades in non-stick cookware and fire-fighting foam. Since 1998, the chemical company DuPont has faced a number of individual and class action lawsuits in US courts over water contamination and PFOA pollution from their Teflon-producing plant in West Virginia.[33] According to leaked internal documents, DuPont knew about the toxic health effects of PFOA since 1961 and about PFOA in the water supply since 1984, but they did not inform workers or the local community. In 2017, the company settled 3,550 individual cases for $671 million.[34] Since 2013, Teflon-branded products have stopped using PFOA, but many PFAS chemicals, a broader class of chemicals, are still in use around the world. PFOA was added to the Stockholm Convention on Persistent Organic Pollutants by the Conference of the Parties in 2019, a global treaty which entered into force in 2004 'to protect the environment and health from chemicals that remain intact in the environment for long periods, become widely distributed geographically, accumulate in the fatty tissue of humans and wildlife, and have harmful impacts on human health or on the environment'.[35]

When petrochemical corporations have lost markets due to toxicity concerns, as in the case of PFOA non-stick coatings, they have filled the gap through marketing substitutions with similar chemical properties, for example short-chain PFAS.[36] While the idea of substituting toxic substances with non-toxic ones is a good one in principle, the problem is that substitutions typically mimic not only the positive chemical properties of the originals (e.g., non-stick or flexible) but also the negative ones (e.g., carcinogenic or mutagenic). As environmental sociologist Phil Brown and his colleagues explain, in the case of PFAS chemicals 'scientists and the public are playing a catch-up game, as older chemicals are phased out and replaced with newer, but similar ones … . Corporations are protected from sharing names of chemicals in new products and mixtures, making it difficult or impossible for scientists to study the new replacements.'[37] The legal basis for this lack of transparency is both unfair and unsafe, benefiting corporations at the cost of people's health.

Denying risk and manufacturing uncertainty are key corporate strategies for protecting markets from threats, particularly when it comes to toxic hazards. However, in the face of other existential threats to business, such as public pressure to address climate change and plastic waste, corporations cannot rely purely on defensive strategies. Instead, they are homing in on the solutions in order ensure future growth. They have been doing this for decades in the case of recycling.

Expanding Markets

In March 2020, as the first wave of COVID-19 was sweeping around the world, the American Public Broadcasting Service (PBS) aired *Plastic Wars*, a joint investigation by PBS Frontline and National Public Radio. With testimonies from industry insiders and documents from corporate archives, the documentary revealed how oil, gas, and plastics companies have promoted recycling for decades, in order to sell more plastics. Faced with a growing public backlash against plastic products in the 1980s, the industry created the Council for Solid Waste Solutions, which piloted recycling programmes and established a code for distinguishing between different kinds of plastic. As the journalist Laura Sullivan reported: 'That code was a numbering system put inside the well-known symbol for recycling – the chasing arrows ♳. The problem, recyclers said, is that it left the impression that all those kinds of plastics were actually being recycled.' Industry leaders campaigned for laws in different US states to be passed mandating the use of these recycling codes ♳ ♴ ♵ in plastic packaging. However, internal corporate documents showed that they knew that most of these products would not be recycled. As one corporate document reported: 'There is "serious doubt" widespread plastic recycling "can ever be made viable on an economic basis"'.[38]

When industry leaders were accused of misleading the public, they insisted that the recycling codes merely identified different types of plastic to assist with recycling, rather than promising that they would be recycled. Government regulators sided with industry, and the codes remained. One former recycling manager who ran recycling centres in Southern California in the 1980s and 1990s reflected on the implications of these policies:

> All of a sudden, our own customers, they would bring it in and not only say it has the triangle, but it would – they would flat-out say, 'It says it's recyclable right on it.' And I'd be like, 'I can tell you, I can't give this away. There's no one that would even take it if I paid them to take it.' That's how unrecyclable it was.[39]

Plastic Wars questioned long-held societal assumptions about recycling as the solution to waste, and it could have had a major impact on public perceptions of the plastics industry. However, the timing was unfortunate, released as the global outrage over plastics was subsiding, overshadowed by the onset of the pandemic. Nonetheless, the message of the documentary did not slip the attention of industry. Tony Radoszewski, president and CEO of the Plastics Industry Association (PLASTICS), issued a statement on the day after the programme aired, dismissing the 'stories that were told' in the documentary as 'misleading', and defending plastic as a 'sustainable material'. Radoszewski also took pains to distance the plastics industry from the statements of two prominent industry insiders, by relegating their views to the past:

> The program included interviews with Lew Freeman and Larry Thomas. We feel that the sentiments of these two former Society of the Plastics Industry (SPI) employees do not reflect the position and attitude of PLASTICS and the plastics industry. At PLASTICS, we are focused on innovation and solving our recycling challenges. Innovation is the hallmark of our industry. We can't speak for anyone who's no longer a part of our organization, or no longer a part of the industry. But

today we know that the plastics industry has nothing to hide – nor does PLASTICS.[40]

Another industry representative, Matthew Naitove, executive editor for *Plastics Technology*, wrote a more indignant response to the programme:

> I've calmed down now, but I was fuming after viewing 'Plastic Wars' on TV Tuesday night, March 31. … As if it had unearthed a new 'DaVinci Code', the film breathlessly announced a theory that plastics recycling is little more than a decades-old scam or distraction of public opinion while the chemical industry covered the earth and clogged the seas with its ever-expanding output of throw-away packaging.[41]

For industry, the suggestion that it had conspired to deceive the public hit a nerve. It flew in the face of its attempts to embrace the twenty-first-century ethos of the 'new' corporation of 'doing well by doing good'.[42] If recycling was questioned by the public, what next?

Yet the findings were not new. In *Plastic: A Toxic Love Story*, published in 2011, Susan Freinkel discussed the issue of the recycling codes and chasing arrows ♲ at length. Freinkel also interviewed industry executives who were frank about their use of psychology in promoting recycling, the aim being to relieve consumer guilt about buying disposable products. In one telling quote, an industry representative called recycling a 'guilt eraser'.[43] Another book from 2011, Samantha MacBride's *Recycling Reconsidered*, shed light on the paradox of recycling, drawing on the author's years of experience managing municipal recycling in New York City. MacBride raised an important question: had the success of the recycling movement diverted attention from environmental problems of waste and overproduction? Unfortunately, she concluded, it had: 'At the inception of the contemporary recycling movement, industrial groups under threat discovered that they could distract civil society and send it in harmless directions.'[44] Despite the altruistic desires of the recycling movement, MacBride showed that their solutions were repeatedly thwarted and co-opted by affected industries.

For the most part, at least until recently, recycling has been accepted by environmental activists and the public as the solution to plastic waste. In 1978, a barge loaded with over 3,100 tons of waste from New York's Long Island came into the media spotlight as a symbol of the escalating waste problem due to the lack of landfill space. The barge, known as the *Mobro 4000*, was turned away from port after port: first in North Carolina, then Louisiana, Texas, and Belize, finally returning to be incinerated and buried in New York.[45] At the height of the media uproar, Greenpeace climbed onto the barge and put up a huge banner that said, 'Next Time ... Try Recycling'. In *Plastic Wars*, Annie Leonard, executive director at Greenpeace, reflected with some regret about the missed opportunity of this moment:

> I think we were naïve. I think we were overly optimistic about the potential of recycling, and perpetuating that narrative led us astray. I mean, absolutely society wide we bought this myth that recycling will solve the problem and we don't need to worry about the amount of plastic being produced.

Leonard is right: the amount of plastic being produced is the real problem. Many others have observed this simple and obvious point.[46] But while the problem is easy to identify, the solutions are not. Recycling remains the favoured solution of industry because it leaves production levels unchallenged. Reducing plastics production, on the other hand, threatens the very basis for capitalist accumulation. After all, the pursuit of profits through expanding markets is the guiding imperative of capitalism.

The massive petrochemical build-out following the US shale gas revolution in the mid-2000s is a case in point, in which the United States emerged as a world leader in oil and gas production. Shale gas exploration opened up abundant reserves of gas from hydraulic fracturing (fracking), a controversial process of extracting gas through injecting high-pressure liquid into subterranean rocks. Fracking involves large amounts of water, toxic chemicals, and heavy equipment. A number of researchers have documented the negative environmental and health impacts of fracking, including land and groundwater contamination, excessive water consumption, air pollution, earth tremors, and high greenhouse gas emissions (particularly from methane).[47] Fracked shale gas has driven hundreds of unsustainable petrochemical expansion projects in the US, banking on continually expanding plastics markets.[48] Corporations across the plastics value chain constantly search for cheap virgin feedstocks, new petrochemical projects, and new plastics markets, striving to manufacture demand for their expanding supply.

The frontiers of plastics expansion are global. As Peter Dauvergne argues, corporations have 'strong financial incentives to create – and then expand – markets for nondurable and disposable products'.[49] Dauvergne highlights the case of China's disposable diaper market, which went from almost nothing in 1998 to annual sales of 2 billion diapers per year in 2013, thanks to millions of dollars in advertising campaigns for Pampers as a way to give babies a 'golden sleep'. Over the past few decades, corporations have also aggressively developed markets for sachets, single-use small portions of food or personal care products, to low-income people in Southeast Asia, which now accounts for 50% of the global sachet market and huge volumes of non-recyclable plastic waste.[50] During this period, China has emerged as the

world's largest producer and consumer of petrochemicals, by both volume and value.[51] There have been a
number of accidents from petrochemical explosions in
China, in addition to reports of high levels of petrochemical pollution.[52] These examples underscore the
uneven benefits and consequences of growing plastics
production and consumption. As the next chapter will
discuss, the relentless expansion of plastics around the
world has been enabled further by the unequal international trade in plastic waste.

Corporate Responsibility and 'Wishcycling'

The idea that we are all to blame for the plastics
crisis avoids questions of responsibility. If we are all
equally to blame, then nobody can be held responsible. Media headlines decrying humanity for wreaking
untold environmental devastation abound: 'The planet's
plastic addiction is hurting the planet'; 'Humans are
driving one million species to extinction'; 'Why didn't
we act on climate when we had the chance?' However,
the universal 'we' erases stark inequalities between
powerful corporations and local communities. As Max
Liboiron asks: 'Who is the "We" in the creation
of plastics that end up in the environment?'[53] Their
answer: the corporations.

Not surprisingly, corporations refuse to take the
blame for the plastics crisis. Instead, they pass it down
the supply chain like a hot potato. The CEO of a
controversial planned petrochemical plant in 'Cancer
Alley' in Louisiana told critics that his plant was based
on clean technology, unlike the neighbouring coal plant:
'I don't want my plant covered in that stuff either!'[54]
He added that shipping was the real polluter, due to
emissions from large LNG ships coming in and out of
the facility. In Antwerp, a petrochemical executive who

had been on a number of corporate beach clean-ups blamed transporters for the piles of tiny plastic pellets known as 'nurdles' that were accumulating along the shores.[55] Ultimately, blame loops back to the public. As one plastics executive said, 'I think we still need to work a lot to make people aware that in the end if the plastic bag is on the road it's because someone has left it there.'[56]

Perhaps the most egregious of the corporate blame games is directed towards countries in Southeast Asia and Africa, where the vast majority of marine plastic waste is concentrated. Corporations blame these countries, the same ones that receive international shipments of plastic scrap, for having poor waste management systems. However, as 'good' twenty-first-century corporations, they offer to help find the solutions. During a plastics industry webinar late in 2020, a corporate executive reflected on his pre-pandemic experiences of visiting a polluted beach in Indonesia for a project to stop ocean plastic waste. He highlighted that his company had no operations in the region but chose to go there because 'if we're going to work to solve this problem, we have to go to where some of the greatest challenges are'. Marvelling at the attitudes of the local people, he exclaimed: 'They don't *want* to create a problem. They don't have waste management systems, and they need help creating them.'[57] This raises questions about the power of narratives for shaping corporate world-views. The executive seemed genuinely pleased that his company was playing a role in helping to address the plastics problem, and in some ways, it probably was. But through wilful ignorance – forgetting to consider the role of plastics producers in overwhelming Indonesia with single-use plastic sachets; and remaining detached from the global inequalities and colonial legacies of the plastic waste trade which compelled Indonesia to receive so many shipments, for a start – the executive failed to recognize that plastics and petrochemical corporations such as his own are the ones responsible for the crisis.

The narrative of saving the world with plastics helps to justify the existence of a toxic and polluting industry, not just for the corporations but also for the people who work for them. On balance, they reason, the benefits of plastics outweigh the problems. Corporations across the plastics value chain perpetuate environmental injustice, using narratives of development to appear to be helping rather than destroying communities. Recycling remains the big guilt eraser, based on societal myths about recycling perpetuated by industry. There is even a word for the practice of continuing to put discarded items into the recycling bin, despite knowing that they will most likely end up being burned or dumped: it's called 'wishcycling'.[58]

I am not suggesting that corporations aim to pollute the environment or to poison people. Their aim is simply to maximize profits by creating, protecting, and expanding markets, regardless of the toxic consequences. But, to separate the aims from the consequences is to retreat into fantasy. So yes, as the Danish Plastics Federation says, let's talk realistically about plastic.

3

The Corporate Alliance to (Never) End Plastic Waste

Images of plastic in oceans went viral in December 2017 after millions of people watched the final BBC episode of David Attenborough's *Blue Planet II*. It seems like old news now. So much has happened since the wave of public outcry over plastic in the oceans just a few years ago. The dystopian images and alarming figures have become part of the media landscape: marine wildlife choking in plastic; 11 million metric tonnes of plastic waste entering the ocean every year; shorelines heaving with toxic trash.[1]

The resulting backlash over the marine plastics crisis posed an existential threat to industry. This chapter documents industry's swift and coordinated response. Amidst the public outrage, petrochemical and plastics corporations scrambled to 'make plastic fantastic again' and to take control of regulations.[2] They participated in multiple beach clean-ups, started developing new recycling technologies, and forged cross-industry partnerships. They lobbied regulators to prevent bans on single-use plastics and to curb the ambition of new environmental policies.

As the crisis unfolded, corporations across the plastics value chain seized upon the discourse of the circular economy, an international policy buzzword that promotes 'closing the loop' in industrial systems, aiming to eliminate waste through the reduction, recycling, reuse, and recovery of resources. In January 2018, the European Commission issued the European Strategy for Plastics in a Circular Economy, which included the target to make all plastics recyclable in Europe by 2030. On the same day, Plastics Europe, the biggest plastics lobby group in Europe, launched its own voluntary initiative, Plastics 2030, committing to 'increase circularity and efficiency', focusing on recycling and preventing 'leakage'.[3] One year later, industry leaders launched the Alliance to End Plastic Waste, pledging $1 billion (with a goal of $1.5 billion over five years) to end ocean plastic waste. Nearly thirty corporations joined this cross-value-chain alliance, including petrochemical companies Shell, Dow, BASF, and ExxonMobil, and the consumer goods giant Procter & Gamble.[4]

Industry recognized a loophole: while the circular economy appears to threaten business as usual, challenging 'take-make-waste' linear models of industrial growth, it doesn't actually limit growth. In most business-led circular economy models for plastics, 'reduction' is interpreted only in terms of reducing 'leakage' and increasing efficiency (through lightweight materials). Production remains untouched.

Thus, the radical potential of the circular economy for plastics is confined to the technological realm. It relies on developing risky new recycling technologies (i.e., chemical recycling) to use recycled plastics instead of 'virgin' fossil fuels as raw material inputs for petrochemical production. And guess who has the cutting-edge expertise to develop these new technologies? Industry's top scientists and engineers have been busy exploring the research possibilities. However, they face serious concerns about the toxic hazards and climate implications for scaling up their fledging technologies. In the meantime, corporations can buy time to continue making plastics from fossil fuels.

Despite the bad press about plastics throughout 2018, industry forecasts for global plastics markets remained optimistic.[5] In fact, the petrochemical industry unveiled plans for unprecedented fossil fuel-based expansion. Between 2008 and 2018, petrochemical corporations in the United States invested more than $200 billion in 333 petrochemical projects linked to fracked shale gas.[6] New mega crude-oil-to-chemicals (COTC) projects, with ten times the capacity of existing world-scale petrochemical plants, were scheduled to start operations in China and Saudi Arabia.[7] In 2019, Hengli Petrochemical's complex in Dalian, China, became one of the world's first COTC mega-projects to come online.[8]

Since the Alliance to End Plastic Waste was launched, it has drawn fierce criticism from environmental organizations for the gap between its multibillion-dollar petrochemical investments and its $1.5 billion commitment to cleaning up waste.[9] Unfazed, the Alliance has continued its work of keeping the conversation focused on waste, gradually expanding its corporate membership. Its website features bold statements that pan across a clear blue sky full of birds, to a pristine ocean, to a hand grasping a plastic bottle from the water: 'Ending plastic waste is an ambitious vision. But we can do it if the world works together. Because together, we can make a difference.'[10] This brings us back to the question: who is this 'we'? And why set such an unachievable goal?

It depends on what counts as success. The political and economic ambitions of the Alliance go beyond greenwashing. China's National Sword policy came into force in March 2018, banning the import of plastic waste and sending the global recycling system into chaos.[11] In the aftermath of China's ban, the Alliance has adopted a geopolitical role in facilitating the global waste trade in South and Southeast Asia, through partnerships with international and national development organizations. This involves exporting risky new technological solutions for managing plastic waste, which links to debates about 'waste colonialism', the term many activists and politicians have used to describe the unequal international trade in hazardous waste.[12]

The marine plastics crisis has lost some of its power to shock, eclipsed by the even greater devastation of the climate emergency and the COVID-19 pandemic. The public mood may have shifted, but the dust has not yet settled. It is important now to reflect on that most recent period of public awakening to the plastics crisis, to understand the stakes that were raised, the barriers to systemic change that were exposed, and the urgency of the collective work that has yet to be done.

The Marine Plastics Crisis

The crisis was a long time coming. The first reports of seabirds and seals entangled with ocean plastic debris emerged in the 1960s.[13] Throughout the 1970s, scientists became increasingly concerned about the ecological impacts of marine plastic pollution. Industry leaders initially denied the problem, insisting that plastics were 'a minor component of the total refuse' in the ocean.[14] However, by the 1980s, they could no longer deny the issue. Instead, they argued that plastic pollution was uncontrollable, and that industry could not be held responsible for the disposal of consumer end products.[15] Faced with rising public pressure, the plastics industry began to invest in recycling programmes and ran advertisements emphasizing individual consumer responsibility for recycling.

In 1997, a large concentration of floating marine plastic debris was found in the North Pacific Ocean, drawing international attention to the scale of the plastics crisis. The discovery of this Great Pacific Garbage Patch, a soupy mixture twice the size of Texas, made it clear that poor waste management on land was a major source of ocean pollution. Environmental activists began to draw connections between plastic waste problems on the land and the sea, starting in South Asia.[16] In the late 1990s, local communities in Bangladesh and India protested for tighter regulations of plastic bags, which clogged sewer drains, contributing to flood risks. Bangladesh was the first country to ban thin plastic bags in 2002 after a deadly flood in 1998.

A number of national, regional, and municipal governments around the world followed suit. South Africa, Taiwan, and Ireland introduced legislation to restrict plastic bags in the early 2000s, and San Francisco became the first US city to ban plastic bags in 2007.[17] The petrochemical and plastics industries fought vehemently to defend their markets. They conducted lifecycle analyses to show that plastic bags were more environmentally friendly than paper and more sanitary than reusable bags. In the United States, the industry-backed 'Save the Plastic Bags Coalition' sued municipalities for failing to conduct environmental assessments prior to implementing bans. Some corporations also offered funding for municipal recycling programmes, but only if cities agreed to back down on plastics legislation. As the political economist Jennifer Clapp argues, the threat of litigation resulted in a 'regulatory chill' that undermined local communities' efforts to curb plastic pollution.[18]

In spite of corporate lobbying, governments around the world continued to introduce legislation to restrict single-use plastics throughout the 2010s, including bans on bags, bottled water, microbeads, and straws. An emotive rallying call over marine plastic pollution came in 2015 when marine biologist Christine Figgener posted a video of an injured sea turtle with a plastic straw stuck up its nose.[19] The video went viral and became a symbol of the growing anti-plastics movement, leading to a number of plastic straw bans around the world.

For all of this momentum, the intensity of the public outrage over the marine plastics crisis in 2017 and 2018 was a critical turning point. It's difficult to say why it hit such a nerve. Perhaps it was the visceral imagery of dying wildlife, or the disturbing confrontation with consumer guilt. Perhaps it fed off the deepening anxieties of the post-truth age. Whatever the cause, plastic waste saturated media headlines and policy discussions, and rocketed to the top of corporate agendas.

'This is the first major disruption that the industry has witnessed,' a petrochemical executive told me. 'Instead of a technological disruption, it is a social disruption.'[20] The executive had a short memory, I thought, recalling the toxic scandals. But I took his point. Negative public perceptions threatened the industry's 'social licence to operate.' With increasing bans on single-use plastics and ambitious new recycling targets, identifiable plastics markets would be affected. This was indeed a major disruption.

Yet it was also an opportunity. Times of crisis call for solutions. Industry will always oppose bans, but recycling is something they can get behind. As we discussed in chapter 2, industry has a long history of co-opting recycling initiatives to ensure that recycling does not threaten production. Enter the circular economy.

The Circular Economy Solution

Within just a few years, the concept of the circular economy has become a dominant corporate sustainability discourse. The Ellen MacArthur Foundation, a UK charity launched in 2010, has led the global business case for the circular economy 'based on the principles of designing out waste and pollution, keeping products and materials in use, and regenerating natural systems'.[21] Within the corporate world, momentum behind the circular economy picked up in 2013 when the Foundation established a network of 100 global corporations, the 'Circular Economy 100'. The Foundation also advised the European Commission, which unveiled its own Circular Economy Action Plan in 2015, identifying plastics as a key priority area. Since then, the idea of the circular economy has gradually permeated global corporate and policy sustainability discourses, rippling across interconnected industries and value chains.

At the World Economic Forum in Davos in 2016 and 2017, the Ellen MacArthur Foundation and the World Economic Forum launched two successive reports on *The New Plastics Economy*, outlining a transition strategy for the plastics industry towards a circular economy.[22] As the marine plastics crisis was escalating, the European Commission launched its Strategy for Plastics in a Circular Economy in January 2018. The strategy document encouraged industry to 'make voluntary commitments in support of the strategy's objective, in particular as regards the uptake of recycled plastics', and to improve cooperation across the value chain on product design and the development of a global protocol for plastics.[23] Plastics industry associations did make voluntary commitments, but they were less ambitious than the Commission, ironically framing their commitments in terms of their 'ambition' to increase reuse and recycling for plastic packaging, without making firm commitments. In May 2018, the Corporate Europe Observatory released a leaked early draft of the European Commission's Strategy for Plastics, showing that the Commission had tried, but failed, to gain official industry endorsement for the strategy.[24] Despite having had significant input into the European Strategy for Plastics, industry remained opposed to the specific recycling and reuse targets, and also wanted to avoid opening the door to binding regulations.

In January 2019, I attended a plastics industry event in Antwerp, which the organizers had timed to coincide with the launch of the Alliance to End Plastic Waste. The industry was still reeling from the plastics crisis, and the circular economy was all the rage. 'I think we have lost the mandate from the consumer that plastic is fantastic,' said one corporate representative.[25] Another added: 'To make plastic fantastic again, we need to get it out of the environment and make it circular.' The good news, according to an industry analyst, was that global demand for plastics was rising. The bad news was that 'clearly we have the threat that we cannot continue with virgin resins'. Over the preceding year, corporations across the plastics value chain had hastily signed up to a number of circular economy schemes and worked to design recyclable packaging, develop quality standards, and create new systems for recycling. Many had bought recycling companies or entered into partnerships with waste management firms. But the biggest petrochemical news in Europe that week was actually about growth: the petrochemical giant INEOS announced a €3 billion investment in the Port of Antwerp, the first European petrochemical investment on that scale in decades.[26] In fact, the mood at the event was rather buoyant.

By this time, the top players in the petrochemical and plastics industries had incorporated the circular economy discourse. Tellingly, many corporations reframed their existing corporate sustainability concepts and practices rather than developing new ideas. BASF applied the circular economy idea to its concept of *Verbund*, a design principle of integrated and efficient industrial complexes, and Mitsubishi adapted the circular economy to its concept of KAITEKI, 'sustainable well-being of people, society, and our planet Earth'. On the one hand, this was a functional manoeuvre, to respond to the backlash over the plastics crisis and to comply with new circular economy policies. On the other hand, it was strategic, aiming to contain the potential threat of the circular economy discourse.

The industry was particularly worried about more radical approaches to the circular economy which focus on 'reduction' and 'zero waste'.[27] In her 2019 book *Waste*, political scientist Kate O'Neill contrasts competing visions of the circular economy between waste diversion by corporate elites and waste prevention by zero waste activists.[28] For example, Break Free From Plastic, the global movement against plastic pollution that started in 2016, has its own blueprint for a circular economy oriented around zero waste communities. This points to the paradox of the circular economy: for all its flaws, it has the potential to transform the global economy to reduce the harmful effects of waste. Yet there is a high risk of regulatory capture when corporations succeed in controlling the economic and technological pathways forward.

Early proposals for a circular economy in Europe aimed for a 'zero waste' commitment, but due to corporate lobbying, the 2015 Circular Economy Action Plan was scaled back to a tepid pledge to 'minimize waste'.[29] Throughout 2017, the plastics industry lobbied the European Commission on its forthcoming Strategy for Plastics, opposing bans and binding regulations.[30] The final Strategy for Plastics stipulated that the new plastics economy would 'fully respect reuse, repair and recycling needs', but like industry, it neglected to mention 'reduce' beyond the context of waste.[31]

Recently, the Ellen MacArthur Foundation has pushed back against narrow corporate interpretations of the circular economy, calling on businesses to 'put the same amount of effort, ambition level, and investment in solutions that go beyond recycling, solutions that reduce the need for single-use packaging in the first place, to rethink and redesign production and consumption models'.[32] In October 2018, it launched the New Plastics Economy Global Commitment, in collaboration with the United Nations Environment Programme (UNEP), focusing on the elimination of problematic plastic packaging at source, in addition to Extended Producer Responsibility (EPR) requirements for producers to bear financial responsibility for the full lifecycle of plastic products. Despite adopting the circular economy discourse, the major plastics producers have been conspicuously absent from the corporate signatories to the Global Commitment: as of 2020, only seven plastics producers, representing 4.4% of global plastics production, had signed up.[33]

The extent of collaboration across the plastics value chain over the marine plastics crisis has been impressive in terms of both speed (within months) and scope (from oil and petrochemical majors to plastics converters to big retail brands to waste management companies). Early in 2019, I spoke with a catalyst engineer from a leading petrochemical company, who told me that she had been on a number of beach clean-ups in Texas and that all the companies were doing the same things.[34] She said that the most inspiring lesson that she had learned through engaging in circular economy debates was the importance of collaboration rather than competition among different companies, which was unprecedented. She had been working in the industry for more than thirty years and characterized it as highly competitive, with intense rivalries between leading companies over patents. But the stakes were high: if they didn't cooperate on making compatible recycling standards and waste streams, then they wouldn't be able to operate, so their business strategies for adapting their systems to meet recyclability goals depended on collaboration. The alternative, she said, was leaving it to the regulators.

The Promise and Peril of Chemical Recycling

Since absorbing the circular economy discourse, corporations have sought to extend their markets through providing the technological solutions to meet new circular economy demands for recycled plastics. The problem, according to industry experts, is that the supply of recycled plastics cannot keep up with demand.[35] Rather than reducing the global production of plastics, they propose to recycle plastics on an unprecedented scale through developing chemical recycling. By pushing for a type of recycling that is still in an early developmental stage, with significant barriers to economic feasibility, and major questions about its own safety and regulation, the industry can also carve out time in which it can continue to produce virgin plastic.

In March 2019, the European Commission issued a press release confirming that 'three years after adoption, the Circular Economy Action Plan can be considered fully completed'.[36] The 244-page report *A Circular Economy for Plastics* detailed the 'future-proof' plans to implement their flagship Plastics Strategy, drawing on insights from scientific research and innovation, which were drafted in consultation with multiple industry stakeholders from across the plastics value chain. In particular, the report identified the need for new investments in 'high-risk, disruptive innovations', including chemical recycling.[37]

A Circular Economy for Plastics defines chemical recycling as 'any reprocessing technology using chemical agents or processes that directly affect either the formulation of the plastic or the polymer itself'.[38] The rationale behind chemical recycling is that we need to bring plastics back to their molecular chemical levels in order to achieve full recyclability. Current mechanical recycling systems have inherent problems with contamination and poor quality that cannot be fully resolved through product redesign. Contamination is of particular concern for food packaging. The advantage of chemical recycling is that it can produce close to 'virgin-grade' plastics. 'Unbaking the cake' is an analogy that industry has used to explain chemical recycling.[39] A more appropriate one would be 'having your cake and eating it too'.

Most forms of chemical recycling would require large scales of production in order to be cost-effective, which would entail building enormous, expensive, and energy-intensive industrial facilities. There have been debates over whether some forms of chemical recycling (e.g., feedstock recycling) can even be called recycling because they produce fuel and thus count as energy recovery.[40] While pointing to the need for chemical recycling to comply with recycling targets, some industry analysts recognize that the environmental gains are not straightforward because chemical recycling 'has an adverse carbon lifecycle assessment (LCA) footprint'.[41] Owing to their scale and energy intensity requirements, chemical recycling projects (as yet undeveloped) would emit large volumes of greenhouse gases, which would seriously undermine climate policy efforts. Furthermore, industry experts typically downplay issues of toxicity, treating these as technological hurdles. Many forms of chemical recycling, however, produce noxious waste streams including dioxins, particularly for certain types of plastics such as polyester and PVC.[42] None of these problems will be resolved, and some may even be intensified, by the addition of a full-scale chemical recycling industry.

Plastics production, whether based on recycled or new materials, is highly toxic, with health risks and environmental justice consequences across the whole value chain. The health effects from exposure to toxic petrochemicals include cancer, lung disease, neurological damage, and other illnesses.[43] The most polluting petrochemical factories around the world are located next to low-income, ethnic-minority, and working-class communities, following global patterns of environmental injustice. Residents and workers in many of these petrochemical communities have endured struggles with toxic pollution and environmental hazards.[44]

The technocratic language of chemical recycling masks the potential environmental justice consequences of its development. Over a decade ago, environmental justice scholar David Pellow argued that the global hazardous waste trade was premised on 'a racist and classist culture and ideology within northern communities and institutions that view toxic dumping on poor communities of color as perfectly acceptable'.[45] Pellow's key example of this ideology was an internal World Bank memo written in 1991 by then chief economist and vice president Lawrence Summers, in which he presented an economic case for dumping international toxic waste in Africa:

> Shouldn't the World Bank be encouraging MORE migration of the dirty industries to the LDC [lesser developed countries]? I can think of three reasons. ... (1) A given amount of health impairing pollution should be done in the country with the lowest cost, which will be the country with the lowest wages. I think

the economic logic behind dumping a load of toxic waste in the lowest wage country is impeccable and we should face up to that. (2) I've always thought that under-populated countries in Africa are vastly UNDER-polluted, their air quality is probably vastly inefficiently low compared to Los Angeles or Mexico City. (3) The concern over an agent [pollutant] that causes a one in million change in the odds of prostate cancer is obviously going to be much higher in a country where people [actually] survive to get prostate cancer than in a country [with higher mortality rates].[46]

This memo sparked extensive media coverage and public discussion, and it remains an infamous reference point within the history of global environmental justice. However, the World Bank refused to reconsider the economic rationale behind the memo, which has continued to guide its international development policies, including many toxic technology transfer schemes.[47]

A similar – if more coded – statement about chemical recycling has recently been published, rather than leaked, by a key industry analyst for the petrochemical industry:

For plastics recycling to be financially attractive, there must be a workable margin for everyone in the recycling chain – including municipalities, sorters, processors, and mechanical and chemical recyclers. And the best solution may vary by geography. The mega-cities of China could favor an approach for polyester linked to the existing gasification infrastructure. In Europe, certain major cities are located near petrochemical production, which may lead them to polyethylene pyrolysis for liquids cracking.[48]

The euphemism that the 'best solution may vary by geography' offers a clue about the injustice that lies behind this statement. However, to understand the environmental justice implications, one would need to know that polyester presents particularly hazardous toxic issues for chemical recycling and also requires incredibly large scales for production. In comparison, polyethylene pyrolysis is relatively safe and can be done on smaller scales.[49] The message is thus to export risky, dangerous toxic technologies requiring vast scales of production to the mega-cities of China, while developing relatively small-scale, safe, and tested technologies within Europe.

Business-led circular economy plans fail to account for the environmental justice and climate change implications of new chemical recycling technologies. As Kate O'Neill argues, the risks of waste management as well as waste solutions have magnified, disproportionately affecting vulnerable communities.[50] In fact, many corporate circular economy 'solutions' to the plastics crisis, such as those of the Alliance to End Plastic Waste, are examples of 'waste colonialism'.

Plastics and Waste Colonialism

China's decision to ban all foreign imports of plastic waste in July 2017 exposed the stark global inequalities in plastic waste exports, systemic problems of contaminated plastic scrap, and interdependencies across the global recycling system. Some plastic waste is easily recyclable, valuable, and safe to handle, but the majority is difficult to recycle, low value, and toxic. In high-income countries, the costs of recycling low-value plastic are typically higher than the costs of using virgin plastic, and for decades they have relied on exporting much of their plastic waste to low- and middle-income countries. Between 1992 and 2017, China took in the largest share of the world's plastic scrap, a cumulative 45.1%, to feed its rapidly growing economy.[51] According to historian Joshua Goldstein, plastic recyclers in China were able to profit from this trade due to three factors: (1) low shipping costs of container ships returning to China after unloading shipments of manufactured goods; (2) low wages of labourers in the plastics recycling economy in China; and (3) high demand for raw plastic materials in China.[52] This seemed like a mutually beneficial trade relationship, but the plastic waste economy posed serious environmental and health risks for workers and communities in China, who faced toxic exposures from sorting and burning the waste.

Amid growing concerns about the social and ecological costs of toxic pollution from the plastic scrap economy, China introduced the 'Green Fence' policy in 2013, an effort to improve the quality of plastic waste imports. However, the policy failed to improve the situation. In 2016, Jiu-Liang Wang's documentary *Plastic China* exposed the brutal economic hardships and health risks of recycling plastic waste in rural China. This heart-wrenching film captured international and national public attention and influenced the Chinese government's decision to ban imported plastic waste.[53] China's ban came into effect in March 2018, causing a major disruption to the global recycling system, particularly for high-income countries that had grown dependent on waste exports.[54] At first, the global flows of waste simply changed course, moving to countries in Southeast and East Asia that would accept the tainted shipments. However, it was not long before many of these countries, too, imposed import restrictions, unable to cope with the incredible volumes.

In the ensuing months, media reports abounded with stories of public outrage over rich countries dumping their waste on developing countries.[55] In many ways, this was a familiar story of 'waste colonialism', echoing debates about international toxic waste dumping in the lead-up to the 1989 Basel Convention on Transboundary Movements of Hazardous Wastes and Their Disposal.[56] The Basel Convention was developed to prevent the inequitable disposal of hazardous waste from high-GDP to low-GDP countries. According to environmental justice scholar David Pellow, there are four explanations for the transnational disposal of toxic waste, either through trade or dumping, to communities in the global South: (1) the exponential increase of hazardous waste produced in industrialized nations, alongside increasing environmental regulations, which have increased the costs of waste management; (2) the need for fiscal relief in the global South, rooted in long histories of colonialism and debt, which has led some government officials to accept financial compensation in exchange for toxic dumping within their borders (also known as 'garbage imperialism' or 'waste colonialism'); (3) the logic of economic globalization, whereby toxic wastes are dumped and traded in nations and communities where there will be the greatest profit; and (4) a dominant ideology of environmental racism and classism, exemplified by the infamous World Bank memo that promoted toxic dumping in Africa.[57]

In May 2019, 186 national governments approved an amendment proposed by Norway to the Basel Convention which expanded the definition of hazardous waste to include most types of plastic waste.[58] Faced with legislative hurdles and accumulating piles of plastic scrap, the top plastics-exporting countries have since tried to overhaul their recycling systems and technologies, but they have not been able to deal with their own volumes of waste. Instead of shipping their unwanted plastic waste to China, they have sent much of it to incinerators and landfills.[59] Yet they have not given up on exporting their plastic waste. The amended Basel Convention contains loopholes, like the original one, whereby importers can agree to accept waste through 'prior informed consent'.[60]

While there have been many discussions of toxic dumping following China's ban, less attention has been paid to the devastating loss of livelihoods for millions of informal waste workers.[61] Adam Minter, author of *Junkyard Planet*, has pushed back against 'the persistent idea that developed countries "dump" their recyclable and re-usable discards on developing countries'.[62] Minter argues that this view ignores the fact that waste is purchased by developing countries, and that when people use the term 'dumping', they 'implicitly deny agency to the highly sophisticated trading and processing businesses that operate across the developing world'.[63] Indeed, it is important to recognize that there are distinctions between trading and dumping, even though many recyclable plastics that are traded legally are later dumped illegally. It is also important to acknowledge the diverse range of experiences, skills, and practices involved in the waste economy. Yet in spite of these complexities, the unequal international trade in plastic waste is still deeply tied to waste colonialism.

In fact, waste colonialism is both wider and more particular than toxic trade and dumping. Max Liboiron argues that waste colonialism is based on the assumption that Land[64] can be used as a sink:

> The assumed entitlement to use Land as a sink, no matter where it is, is rooted in colonialism. Regulatory limits to pollution, which allow some degree of pollution to occur so long as it is below a legislated quantity, are colonialism because they make Land pollutable to begin with. The way waste and toxicities interrupt, damage, and even destroy Indigenous ways of being and relating to Land is colonialism. The extraction of oil and natural gas from Land to create plastic and paper disposables is colonialism. Recycling, incineration, and other waste

managements that 'take care' of waste so that the extraction and access to Land can continue is colonialism. Exporting these models to other places and then blaming the local people for not properly managing colonial sinks is colonialism.[65]

In this insightful passage, Liboiron draws attention to multiple forms of colonialism that underpin assumed entitlement to use Land as a sink. These forms of colonialism include not only exporting waste, but also exporting waste management models and blame. This brings us to the subject of the Alliance to End Plastic Waste.

The Trials of the Alliance

On first glance, the corporate-led Alliance to End Plastic Waste seems like an easy target for criticism, and, indeed, when it was first announced with great fanfare in January 2019, it was widely attacked by environmental organizations. The Dutch–Belgian NGO Recycling Netwerk (*sic*) wryly observed that the Alliance was 'like a who's who of companies investing in the expansion of plastic production'.[66] Similarly, a spokesperson for Greenpeace scoffed: 'Make no mistake, plastics are a lifeline for the dying fossil fuel industry, and this announcement goes to show how far companies will go to preserve it.'[67] Environmentalists around the world proclaimed that it was nothing more than a greenwashing attempt by multinationals to protect petrochemical investments, shift blame onto consumers, and direct attention to waste management rather than the source of the problem.[68]

I agree with these criticisms, but I think that there is more to the Alliance than meets the eye. Its corporate sustainability mission is not just talk. It has real-world implications, making a number of development interventions in heavily polluted and marginalized local communities in Southeast Asia and Africa. At the launch event broadcast in London, leading CEO co-founders presented the 'facts' of the problem of plastic waste: nearly 80% of plastic in the oceans comes from land-based sources, and 60% of that plastic waste comes from just five countries in Southeast Asia, so this was where they were going to start.[69] The CEOs also highlighted a more dubious 'fact': that substituting plastics in packaging with alternative materials would have an environmental impact that would be four times higher than plastics.[70] With their facts assembled, they cautioned against the 'unintended consequences' of substituting plastics and unveiled their grand vision for ending 'unmanaged' plastic waste.

The Alliance operates by seconding experts from across the plastics value chain, particularly the waste management sector, to lead 'catalytic' solution-based projects in different communities. These solutions focus on four key areas: infrastructure, innovation, education and engagement, and clean-ups. Given its strong focus on international development, the Alliance works through partnerships with international and national development agencies, such as UN-Habitat and the United States International Development Agency, in additional to local NGOs.

Now, I don't dispute the possibility that many of these projects could help local communities to build capacity and infrastructure to begin to address seemingly insurmountable plastic waste problems. Nor do I suggest that the people working on these projects aren't trying to help. However, I want to draw our attention to the wider political and economic ambitions of the Alliance, which are deeply rooted in waste colonialism. These ambitions also link to chemical recycling.

Through projects in Southeast Asia and Africa, the Alliance offers corporations opportunities to trial and scale up potentially risky new recycling technologies. It presents these technologies as fully reliable and scalable solutions. According to a senior adviser to the Alliance, 'We already know where the unmanaged plastics are. We already know what the solutions are. It's just a matter of making it commercially viable, making sure the technology can be scaled up with speed into those areas.'[71] The Alliance website includes a section with 'requests for proposals' specifically asking for project proposals based on chemical recycling technologies. Within the geopolitical context of the international trade in plastic waste, this paves the way both for further toxic disposal of waste and for experiments in scaling up solutions.

The top pollution hotspots where the Alliance has focused most of its efforts – Thailand, Vietnam, Indonesia, the Philippines, and India – also happen to be countries that were overwhelmed with imports of plastic waste after China's ban in 2018. In the lead-up to the Conference of the Parties at the Basel Convention in May 2019, the World Plastics Council, an international trade association representing the major plastics producers, issued a strong statement opposing the proposed Norwegian amendment for plastic waste to be classified as 'restricted wastes', requiring prior written consent from importing and transit countries. The Council argued that work was 'already underway to deliver solutions to a waste-free future. CEOs from our industry have launched an unprecedented effort to help end plastic waste in the environment.'[72] They went on to outline the work of the Alliance in leveraging investment in waste management infrastructure, highlighting the benefits of new technologies for accelerating solutions. At the same time, they argued that the proposed amendment 'could create a barrier to innovative new technologies such as chemical recycling which are being developed specifically to recover some mixed or contaminated plastic wastes'. The Council concluded by reiterating the importance of chemical recycling for developing waste solutions in nations that import waste.

In May 2019, the Conference of the Parties approved the amendment to the Basel Convention, which was heralded as a success by environmental organizations and activists. However, the amendment to the Basel Convention did not, as the World Plastics Council warned, stop the drive by powerful corporations – exemplified by the Alliance – to invest in chemical recycling solutions in those unspecified nations that import plastic waste.

Nonetheless, with requirements for written consent from waste-importing countries, the Basel Convention did highlight the imperative for corporations to sell the value of plastic waste.

The Real Value of Plastic Waste

'Now a lot of people don't know that plastic waste actually has value,' explained Bob Patel, CEO of the petrochemical multinational LyondellBasell, at the Alliance's launch event broadcast from London. 'The key is unlocking that value and bringing it back to a useful form again. By tackling plastic waste, we can also impact communities in a very positive way, and people's lives in a very positive way. It can be a means of commerce in different parts of the world.'[73] During a corporate sustainability event held in South Africa early in 2020, a senior adviser from Dow seconded to the Alliance quantified that value:

> We've got to start to turn this problem into an oppor-
> tunity. And so what we've seen is that this 8 million

tons [of plastic waste leaking into the oceans every year] is close to 120 billion tons [*sic*] of value if you direct it and address it differently. And if you can liberate certain continents like Africa, in supporting this $120 billion, that $120 billion can be better directed towards infrastructure, or health care, et cetera.[74]

By advancing this perspective, the industry is selling the idea to vulnerable communities in Africa and Southeast Asia that the toxic waste they are burdened with actually has tremendous value that can simply be 'unlocked' through technological solutions. This is waste colonialism with a corporate sustainability twist. The fantastical accounting hides the fact that most of the technological solutions on offer have not been tested or scaled. It also exploits the 'education and engagement' mission to promote the industry's own version of facts about plastics.

Indeed, the educational mission of the Alliance is one of its most colonial undertakings, echoing the civilizing missions of the past five centuries of European colonialism. The Alliance aims to educate local people and campaign to change their behaviour, following the long-standing corporate narrative that holds individual consumers responsible for plastic waste. It also frames poor waste infrastructure, including uncapped and illegal dumpsites, in terms of education, but on a societal level. As the senior adviser to the Alliance explained:

The fundamental common areas or challenges in developing markets, whether it's Southeast Asia or Africa, is exactly the same, it's the infrastructure. And there is a behavioural aspect which is the education … it's also the behavioural aspect to create infrastructure, create a business model, create employment. I think activating the informal sector in this area is the biggest opportunity to unleash a solution to this prevailing problem.[75]

In the promotional video 'Closing the Loop in Accra, Ghana', posted online in February 2021, a plastic waste picker in Accra reflects on what she has learned by working with a recycling and women's empowerment project through the Alliance:

> At first when I saw plastic sachets in the streets I didn't know of its value, but now I know it can be recycled into another thing which is helping me a lot. So now when I see these sachets I pick them up and even advise people of the essence of those sachets and how best it could help them.[76]

Another waste picker in Accra echoed this revelation: 'Now I walk through the streets and I don't see plastic as trash, I see it as money and so I put value on it.'

The irony of these 'educational' insights is that for years the plastics industry has flooded countries in Africa and Southeast Asia with non-recyclable single-portion sachets. Unilever developed the first recycling technology solution to recycle sachets in 2017 and built a pilot plant in Indonesia in 2018 to test it out, but this recycling technology has not yet been commercialized at the time of writing.[77] The project in Accra relies instead on a different recycling solution, based on a collaboration between the Alliance and the ASASE Foundation, a local social enterprise, which according to the Alliance's 2020 progress report 'empowers women by enabling them to start their own businesses: collecting and recycling plastic waste as a source of much-needed income'.[78] The plastic waste is collected by women on the streets of Accra and then sold to ASASE reprocessing plants that regrind the plastics and sell them to other companies to reuse in other products, such as household or building materials. But does this work? What volumes of waste are recycled in this way? Which companies buy these plastics? Are there issues of toxicity and contamination in their products? How safe is the informal work of waste picking in this project? How viable, sustainable, and ethical is the enterprise?

I raise these questions because they are important to answer in order to evaluate such a project, even on its own terms of community empowerment. However, such information is not readily available beyond the Alliance's report. Owing to the technical expertise involved, it is very difficult for non-experts to know what the risks or benefits are for any given project. In the absence of independent evaluations or insider knowledge, it is impossible to assess the local social and economic consequences of the Alliance's projects in different countries. On the one hand, researchers have raised concerns about the exploitative working conditions and toxic exposures of workers, particularly for women, in the informal waste recycling economy in Africa, as well as in China, South and Southeast Asia, and South America.[79] On the other hand, researchers have highlighted the problem of making assumptions about the working conditions, skills, and technological capacities in such a diverse sector, drawing attention to the significance of the informal waste economy for millions of livelihoods.[80] While it is difficult to assess the local impacts of specific projects, what is clear is that the Alliance is reinforcing an unjust global plastic waste hierarchy, while ensuring that plastics production keeps going and that waste keeps moving in profitable directions.

In January 2021, Reuters reported that one of the Alliance's flagship projects was being terminated. The project was a collaboration with Renew Oceans, a US-based charity dedicated to dredging the Ganges, which had fallen dramatically short of its targets for cleaning up plastic waste. Greenpeace picked up the story, criticizing the Alliance for failing to deliver on its promises to reduce plastic waste.[81] However, the Alliance simply responded by saying that the collaboration with Renew Oceans was just one of their many pilot projects, and that it had stalled due to the pandemic. This easy comeback is the problem with criticizing the Alliance only in terms of its obvious failures, rather than interrogating its wider ambitions and neocolonial success stories.

There are no win-win solutions to the plastic waste crisis. Millions of tons of plastic waste entering the oceans each year cannot magically be converted into billions of dollars without a swathe of destructive impacts. Yes, there is a lot of money to be made from developing plastic waste solutions, but very little of it flows to the vulnerable local communities that are inundated with waste. Instead, the vast majority of it flows to powerful multinational corporations that produce the plastics, sell the solutions, and maintain the unjust international trade in hazardous plastic waste.

4

Hedging Against Climate Risk

While corporations across the plastics value chain have presented an allied front over the plastic waste crisis, they have tried to evade additional scrutiny under the lens of the climate crisis by dissociating themselves from their common roots in oil. Plastics seem to offer a lifeline for oil in the fight against climate change, since they are found in electric cars, wind turbine blades, and energy-efficient building materials. Moreover, global demand for plastics has continued to rise. Fossil fuel-based companies have thus been investing in plastics as a hedge against climate risk. Yet the future of this plastics lifeline remains uncertain as the climate emergency is putting unprecedented pressure on all industries to decarbonize.

In *The Uninhabitable Earth*, the best-selling 2019 'epoch-defining' book about the climate crisis by *New York Magazine* editor David Wallace-Wells, 'plastic panic' is held up as an 'exemplary climate parable, in that it is also a climate red herring'.[1] Wallace-Wells contends that 'while plastics have a carbon footprint, plastic pollution is simply not a global warming problem

– and yet it has slid into the center of our vision, at least briefly, the ban on plastic straws occluding, if only for a moment, the much bigger and much broader climate threat'. This sentiment was also expressed in a 2019 *Marine Policy* article by marine biologist Richard Stafford and geographer Peter J. S. Jones, who wrote that ocean plastic pollution was a 'convenient but distracting truth' from the bigger environmental threats of climate change and biodiversity loss.[2]

In fact, plastic pollution is a major global heating problem, for reasons that I will discuss below. It is also an existential planetary threat, linked to what scientists have termed 'ecological overshoot': population growth and overconsumption beyond the earth's support capacity.[3] Yet what worries me the most about these 'plastic distraction' accounts is that they play into corporate narratives about plastic as an environmentally exceptional use of oil. As a spokesperson for the petrochemical industry explained: 'There are two different ways to work with oil: you can process the oil into a fuel and burn it, or you can put the oil into a chemical plant and refine it and finesse it further into value streams or different kinds of applications like plastics.'[4] Plastics, she reminded me, are in all kinds of high-value, sustainable things.

Plastics are predicted to be the biggest driver of oil demand as the world transitions away from fossil fuels. According to an IEA analyst, the petrochemical industry is an 'exception in the Sustainable Development Scenario', meaning that the industry is expected to profit regardless of global action to meet the Paris climate change targets, due to two parallel trends: increasing plastics consumption in emerging economies; and growing markets for green technologies.[5] However, this expansionary logic is premised on an all-or-nothing approach to plastics production. Even in the Sustainable Development Scenario, involving stronger international climate action and factoring in single-use plastics bans, the largest demand for petrochemicals will continue to be for single-use plastic packaging.

Despite narratives of plastic exceptionalism, global action on climate change is the biggest economic threat facing the petrochemical and plastics industries. In October 2018, the UN Intergovernmental Panel on Climate Change (IPCC) published a stark report warning that the world needs to cut global emissions by half by 2030 and reach zero emissions by 2050, or else face untold climate catastrophe by the end of the century.[6] Decarbonization spells the endgame for fossil fuels, which, as noted in chapter 1, are the raw material basis for 99% of plastics.[7] Many of the biggest plastics producers are vertically integrated oil companies: ExxonMobil, Shell, Saudi Aramco, Sinopec. Their gamble is that plastics don't count as oil. But with investors starting to worry seriously about climate-related risks, all bets are off.

For decades, the oil industry has funded climate change denial and relied on aggressive lobbying to dodge the issue of its contribution to global heating.[8] Meanwhile, the petrochemical and plastics industries have funded studies of plastic bags and other single-use plastic products, which invariably highlight the negative trade-offs with alternative material substitutions.[9] Since 2019, however, corporations have been under increasing pressure to respond to the climate emergency, particularly as a result of climate divestment campaigns and legal requirements by institutional investors and financial institutions (e.g., BlackRock and the Bank of England) for companies to disclose climate risk. Several fossil fuel companies, including BP, Shell, and Total, have pledged to become net zero energy companies by 2050.[10] Echoing the corporate uptake of the circular economy, net zero discourses have rapidly diffused across the plastics value chain. Multinational chemical companies Dow and DuPont, consumer goods corporation Procter & Gamble, and brand retailers Coca-Cola and Nestlé are among the many corporations that have made net zero commitments. The implications of this net zero shift have yet to be seen, but climate pressure shows no signs of abating. The pandemic has strengthened the resolve of many governments to accelerate the transition away from fossil fuels through green recoveries.[11]

Negating the famous quote from *The Graduate*, the green investment think tank Carbon Tracker issued a report in 2020 called *The Future's Not in Plastics*, questioning the oil industry's long-term investment strategy in plastics, which would become stranded assets in the green transition. In the long term, the author of the report said, despite COVID-19, the societal pressures were there to stay: 'Don't forget that plastic is the same as oil, right?'[12] Plastics are indeed oil, and they need to be factored into global green transitions.

Is Plastic Pollution a Global Heating Problem?

Before we revisit the corporate playbook on sowing doubt, let's first address the question: is plastic pollution a global heating problem? Several recent reports suggest that it most certainly is, in contrast to the industry's convenient deflection. And with rising growth in plastics production, it is only going to get worse.

The 2019 report *Plastic and Climate: The Hidden Costs of a Plastic Planet*, co-authored by researchers from the Centre for International Environmental Law (CIEL) and several other environmental organizations, examined the sources of greenhouse gas emissions across every stage of the plastics lifecycle (extraction and transport, refining and manufacture, waste management, and plastic in the environment) for the seven main plastics most commonly found in single-use products.[13] The report estimated that the production and incineration of plastic would add more than 850 million metric tonnes of greenhouse gases to the atmosphere in 2019. This volume would rise to reach 2.8 gigatons of carbon dioxide per year by 2050, with a cumulative total of more than 56 gigatons, or 10–13% of the remaining global carbon budget to stay within the Paris climate change target of 1.5 degrees above pre-industrial levels. The authors also observed that their emissions estimates were 'likely to underrepresent the full emissions profile of the plastic lifecycle'.[14] For example, they cited scientific concerns that microplastics in the ocean interfere with carbon sequestration, pointing to the difficulty of estimating this climate effect with precision.

Another worrying prognosis about plastic-related climate effects was detailed in the 2020 report *Breaking the Plastic Wave* by the Pew Charitable Trusts and SYSTEMIQ, a certified B Corporation ('a new kind of business that balances profit with people and the planet'). The authors of the report used a comprehensive plastic system modelling tool to assess the environmental and socioeconomic implications of the global plastics crisis up until 2040, across a range of different policy scenarios. Their 'Business-as-Usual' scenario predicted that global plastics production would double in capacity by 2040, and that the resulting amount of plastic waste entering the oceans would triple to 29 million metric tonnes per year. Meanwhile, lifecycle plastic-related emissions would rise from 1.0 gigatons of equivalent carbon dioxide ($GtCO_2e$) in 2016 to 2.1 $GtCO_2e$ by 2040, using up 19% of the total remaining global carbon emissions budget to keep heating to 1.5 degrees over the period. One of the authors' key climate findings was that even their proposed 'System Change' scenario would still use up 15% of the global carbon emissions budget, and thus they advised that 'it will be critically important to look beyond the interventions modelled in the scenario' for solutions to reduce plastic-related greenhouse gas emissions.[15]

Similarly, the 2020 report *Reaching Net Zero* by the International Renewable Energy Agency (IRENA) predicted that global plastics production could triple by 2050 and that related emissions could rise to 2.5 gigatons of CO_2 per year by 2050, if current policies continue.[16] The report focused on seven key industrial sectors which face considerable economic and technological hurdles to decarbonization: the four most energy-intensive industries (iron and steel, cement and lime, chemicals and petrochemicals, and aluminium) and three key transport sectors (road freight, aviation, and shipping). In 2017, the chemicals and petrochemicals sector accounted for nearly 5% of total global greenhouse gas emissions (90% of the chemicals sector is in petrochemicals). The authors of the report argued that the full lifecycle of plastic carbon emissions needs to be considered because only direct energy and emissions processes were being counted towards the sector's carbon footprint.[17] Technically, it would be possible for the sector to decarbonize, the authors suggested, through reducing demand for petrochemicals and switching to alternatives to fossil fuel feedstocks. However, they also cautioned that decarbonization would not happen on its own without political intervention due to the high economic costs.

It seems obvious, really, that unfettered plastics production and pollution will lead to a dramatic increase in greenhouse gas emissions. In a 2021 article entitled 'Underestimating the Challenges of Avoiding a Ghastly Future', conservation scientists issued a grim warning about three existential environmental threats to the biosphere and all lifeforms on earth: biodiversity loss, climate disruption, and ecological overshoot. According to the scientists, 'This massive ecological overshoot is largely enabled by the increasing use of fossil fuels. These convenient fuels have allowed us to decouple human demand from biological regeneration: 85% of commercial energy, 65% of fibers, and most plastics are now produced from fossil fuels.'[18] They argued further that without fundamental changes to capitalism, education, and equality, the three existential threats together will accelerate a vicious cycle of ecological deterioration throughout the twenty-first century, involving mass extinction, declining health, large-scale climate migration, and resource conflicts. Their urgent conclusion was that scientists need to be more vocal about their warnings to humanity, for they have thus far been 'insufficiently foreboding to match the scale of the crisis'.[19]

This is despite the foreboding warnings that *have* been voiced by scientists for decades. The *Limits to Growth* report for the Club of Rome, first published in 1972, used a systems modelling approach to analyse the long-term causes and consequences of material and economic growth for the planet.[20] The report found that global ecological constraints related to resource use and emissions would have a significant influence on global developments in the twenty-first century. The authors cautioned that humanity was already on track to overshoot the earth's support capacity. In their twenty-year update, *Beyond the Limits*, they argued that the planet had already reached the point of ecological overshoot and reiterated this even more forcefully in their thirty-year update. *Limits to Growth* had a major influence on debates about how to balance the imperatives for economic growth with those of sustainability.[21] However, the simple idea that growth is limited on a finite planet has been ignored by mainstream politicians, economists, and corporations. So too, until recently, has the idea of taking real action on climate change. But there is a reason that climate scientists, in particular, have been insufficiently foreboding: reprisals from powerful fossil fuel interests.

Degrees of Denial

A common misconception about climate change denial is that the history of denial is as old as the history of acceptance. On the contrary, climate change denial campaigns were initiated by oil companies in the 1980s and 1990s who internally understood and accepted the science of global warming.[22] They also recognized that climate change posed an existential threat to their business. As Naomi Oreskes and Erik Conway document in *Merchants of Doubt*, the oil industry borrowed directly from the Big Tobacco playbook to cast doubt publicly on the science of climate change. Some of the same scientists who were enrolled into the tobacco industry's efforts to manufacture uncertainty about the health effects of smoking were also involved in climate change denial campaigns. One of their most underhand tactics was to personally attack the reputations of leading climate scientists by spreading misinformation about their scientific findings and professional conduct.

For many years, this strategy worked to delay widespread political and public acceptance of climate change, particularly in the United States, despite the overwhelming consensus (97%) of climate scientists around the world. Major oil corporations actively funded climate denial and questioned the legitimacy of scientific research about climate change. However, in recent years, oil and gas corporations have faced widespread public criticism over their role in delaying action to address the climate crisis, resulting in cases of costly climate litigation.

To date, the most infamous case of corporate climate deception is that of ExxonMobil (formerly Exxon). In 2015, reporters from *Inside Climate News* published an exposé about the history of Exxon's engagement with climate science.[23] The authors revealed that Exxon had conducted cutting-edge climate science research in the 1970s and 1980s, which confirmed the growing scientific consensus about the connection between fossil fuels and global warming. However, Exxon executives kept this research quiet. Political attention to climate change rose in the 1980s, culminating in James Hansen's testimony to the US Senate in 1988 that global warming was already underway, the same year that the IPCC was founded. Switching to full defence mode, Exxon abandoned its climate research in the 1990s and turned its attention to a concerted effort to mislead the public in order to delay action on climate change. Together with other major oil companies, such as the American private multinational Koch Industries, Exxon funded climate change denial and uncertainty campaigns through right-wing think tanks, including the Heartland Institute and the Cato Institute.[24] The 2015 media revelations about Exxon led to the #ExxonKnew petition to launch a criminal investigation into the company, and to a series of lawsuits against Exxon for deceiving the public about climate change.

The days of corporate climate change denial, while not over, are increasingly numbered. Funding outright denial is no longer a viable corporate survival strategy for dodging the climate crisis, at least not as the dominant one. Since the Paris Agreement was concluded in 2015, oil and gas corporations have adapted their strategies to play a double-sided game, publicly recognizing the need to address climate change, while lobbying to delay climate action through both overt and covert methods. Over the past decade, oil and gas companies have spent billions of dollars in lobbying to delay and prevent climate legislation.[25] As of January 2020, the IEA reported that less than 1% of the oil and gas industry was invested in renewables, and despite a rhetoric of change, the industry was continuing with fossil fuel exploration.[26] However, the industry has been positioning itself for what it calls the 'decade of delivery' to transform from 'crisis to low-carbon opportunity', particularly in the post-pandemic drive towards green recoveries.[27] One of the lights at the end of the tunnel is plastics.

The top global integrated oil companies, including ExxonMobil, Sinopec, and Saudi Aramco, have been rapidly expanding their virgin plastics production over the past decade, enabled by billions of dollars in investments and loans from investors, banks, and governments.[28] While there has been increasing pressure on these plastics producers to reduce their reliance on virgin fossil fuel feedstocks, there has been very little movement in this direction.[29] Some of the problem is technical, given the lack of developed and scalable alternatives: chemical recycling is still in an early stage of development; bio-based feedstocks are limited in supply; and both of these alternatives are associated with environmental problems of their own. However, most of the problem is economic, due to relatively cheap virgin feedstocks as compared with recycled and bio-based feedstocks. The powerful corporate incumbents also have vested interests in profiting from oil while they still can.

The Plastics Exception

Confronted with the existential threat of the global transition away from fossil fuels, major oil companies have started to diversify into petrochemicals, to hedge their risk of stranded assets. The new COTC mega-projects under development in China and Saudi Arabia testify to the scale of the petrochemical shift. These mega-projects will convert oil directly to petrochemicals, bypassing fuels altogether, and are projected to have ten times the petrochemical capacity of the largest conventional facilities. Despite delays to these developments due to the disruptions of the pandemic, multi-billion-dollar COTC projects have ploughed ahead.[30]

The petrochemical industry historically has been a junior partner to the oil and gas industries, relying on by-products from refining for fuel markets. This relationship is set to change. In March 2021, the International Energy Agency released the report *Oil 2021*, a mid-term forecast for oil markets until 2026 following the collapse of oil demand in 2020 during the pandemic. The report predicted high levels of uncertainty in future oil demand due to increasing government plans to accelerate low-carbon transitions. However, it cautioned against divesting from fossil fuels, arguing that these will be important for preventing supply and price disruptions. Notably, the petrochemical industry was held up as a source of optimism for oil demand: 'The petrochemical industry remains a pillar of growth over the forecast period. Ethane, LPG, and naphtha [petrochemical feedstocks] together account for 70% of the projected increase in oil product demand to 2026.'[31] The findings align with other IEA predictions that petrochemicals are 'rapidly becoming the fastest driver of global oil demand'.[32]

IEA's report *The Future of Petrochemicals*, published in 2018, identifies the petrochemical industry as the world's largest industrial consumer of oil and gas, at 14% and 8%, respectively.[33] The report draws attention to the seeming contradiction that the chemical industry is 'only' the third largest industrial carbon dioxide emitter. It explains that the reason for this gap between fossil fuel consumption and carbon emissions is because oil and gas are used by the industry as feedstocks, in addition to being combusted. The implication is that carbon emissions are saved during plastics production and thus offer benefits in terms of efficiency. Many scientists, energy analysts, and environmental groups have criticized the IEA for making overly optimistic predictions about the future of fossil fuels, while making overly pessimistic predictions about growth in renewable energy sources, suggesting that the IEA has steered investments in favour of fossil fuels rather than alternatives.[34] The IEA's Sustainable Development Scenario has been particularly controversial due to its lack of ambition towards meeting zero net emissions targets and its overall vision of virgin plastics-driven growth.

As another example of creative accounting, the story of shale gas is also linked to the plastics exception. Although natural gas is a fossil fuel, the US shale gas industry positions it as a 'transition fuel', since it burns cleaner as a fuel than coal, with one quarter of the carbon emissions. However, shale gas production releases methane, a more potent greenhouse gas than carbon. When methane emissions are taken into account, the total greenhouse gas emissions of shale gas production are significantly higher than those of conventional natural gas, coal, and oil.[35] Shale gas is also used as a cheap raw material feedstock in plastics production, and thus plastics also offer a hedge for shale gas against the transition to renewables.[36]

How did plastics come to be seen as exceptional in relation to climate change? At the launch of the Alliance to End Plastic Waste in January 2019, the CEO co-founders cited a 2016 study which showed that replacing plastic packaging with alternative materials would have four times the environmental impact of plastics. The study was funded by the American

Chemistry Council and completed by Trucost, a corporate consultancy firm that assesses social environmental risk.[37] The headline findings have been referenced repeatedly by industry representatives. For example, a petrochemical CEO made the following comment at an industry event in 2020:

> Replacing packaging and consumer material could have an environmental cost escalation of near four times. So we have to be very, very careful of the unintended consequences of this shift away from one sustainable, or very, very prudent, or the most effective packaging into another alternative because the environmental burden … four times, four times![38]

This corporate statement has an air of slipperiness about it, shifting from the bold assertion that plastic is a sustainable material to more cautious adjectives, and, finally, just repeating the headline figure, like a politician on the defensive. This constant repetition of the same headline finding from a single industry-backed study raises questions about the reliability of the research. Why have industry representatives relied so heavily on the Trucost study, given there has been a lack of corroboration for its key claims?

In fact, the Trucost study follows a trend of other industry-sponsored lifecycle assessments (LCAs) of plastic products. LCA is a quantitative methodology used by industry and policymakers to evaluate the environmental impacts of products or services across all stages of their lifecycle: for example, studies in the mid- to late 2000s which showed that plastic bags were more environmentally friendly than paper or cotton bags.[39] Corporate LCAs of plastic packaging, including the Trucost study, rely on the assumption that global mass consumption of single-use products will continue, rather than considering the possibility of reusing products or reducing consumption. In the bags studies, for example, the assumption was that alternatives to plastic bags would mean that people would use single-use paper bags instead, rather than making a permanent switch away from single-use bags altogether, or else they would reuse cotton bags, but no more than a handful of times. Through carefully tailoring the parameters and assumptions behind lifecycle analysis, plastics invariably come out as the environmentally friendly solution. Even so, I have not yet seen any corroboration of the Trucost study findings. Perhaps one bespoke favourable study is all the industry needs. As we will discuss in chapter 6, there are of course environmental impacts when substituting single-use plastic packaging with paper, bioplastics, or other materials, but it is far from clear that they are 'four times' worse. The wider point is that producing vast quantities of disposable packaging is unsustainable, regardless of the material.

The petrochemical and plastics industries also claim that plastics are crucial for climate change solutions. On some levels, this is true. Lightweight, versatile, and inexpensive, plastics are widely used for climate mitigation technologies, particularly energy and fuel efficiency. For example, building insulation materials, often made out of foam plastics, save on energy costs for heating and cooling. Wind turbine blades, solar panels, and electric vehicles are made up of composite materials which include plastics. However, the proportion of plastics that goes into green technologies is negligible in comparison with single-use plastic packaging markets. On the packaging front, industry representatives have another line, claiming that lightweight plastic packaging and automotive plastics save on fuel costs for transportation and extend the shelf-life of food products, not to mention being 'four times' more environmentally friendly. The industry has gone further, claiming that, ultimately, the climate benefits of plastics outweigh the costs. In 2009, McKinsey published *Innovations for Greenhouse Gas Reductions*, a report commissioned by the International Council of Chemical Associations, with the key 'lifecycle quantification' finding that chemical industry products save twice the greenhouse gas emissions that are emitted in making the products.[40] Ironically, this lifecycle report failed to take into account the full greenhouse gas-emitting lifecycle of petro-chemical and plastics production, and it obscured the fact that climate mitigation has always been marginal, if not antithetical, to petrochemical markets. Even in its own terms, this kind of carbon accounting appears outdated – and all the more so now, in the context of the race to net zero emissions.

The Reluctant Race to Net Zero

In February 2020, oil and gas representatives from around the world met at the annual IP Week in London as COVID-19 was spreading around the world.[41] The event went ahead as planned, just before the lockdowns in Europe and North America, but several networking meetings were cancelled. The climate emergency was at the top of the agenda, framed in corporate language as a matter of 'ESG': environmental, social, and governance risks. The event tagline was 'The oil and gas industry changed the world before. Can it do it again?'

The keynote address at the IP Week dinner was by Bernard Looney, the new CEO of BP, who spoke of the great speed of change in the energy landscape.[42] His answer to the drive for a low-carbon economy was that Big Oil had to become 'smart oil', using the oppor-tunity of the crisis to overcome cost cycles through digitization, standardization, and simplification. In investment terms, Looney said that BP needed to 'pull back when necessary' in order to stay competitive, citing its 'tough decision' not to pursue oil drilling in the Great Australian Bight. Earlier that month, BP had pledged to have a 'net zero ambition' for 2050, following Repsol's net zero announcement just months before. This led to a number of similar net zero pledges by major European integrated oil and gas companies, including Shell, Total, and ENI – all plastics producers – early in 2020. In November 2020, the American companies Occidental Petroleum and ConocoPhillips also made net zero pledges, putting pressure on the largest US oil majors, ExxonMobil and Chevron, to join the club.[43] At the time of writing in 2021, ExxonMobil has only gone so far as to say it will 'respect and support society's ambition to achieve net zero emissions by 2050'.[44]

Industry analysts and reporters were swift to respond to the net zero pledges from major oil and gas companies, many of which are also leading plastics producers.[45] First, many argued, net zero pledges were framed as 'ambitions' rather than binding targets, and they did not apply equally to different parts of businesses. Second, there were no standards for private-led net zero targets.[46] While some pledges were more wide-ranging than others, virtually all corporate net zero pledges contained loopholes. For example, most pledges excluded 'scope 3' emissions, the indirect emissions from a company's value chain, which account for the vast majority of fossil fuel emissions. Third, all of the major oil and petrochemical companies' net zero strategies appeared to rely heavily on the use of unproven carbon capture and storage (CCS) technologies, rather than the elimination of greenhouse gas emissions.

The rise of the net zero discourse goes beyond the fossil fuel sector. The United Nations launched its global Race to Zero Campaign in June 2020, rallying businesses, cities, regions, and investors to shift towards a decarbonized economy.[47] A number of national and regional governments have made commitments to halve emissions by 2030 and to reach net zero emissions by 2050, responding to global pressure to address the climate emergency in the wake of the IPCC special report *Global Warming of 1.5°C*.[48] In October 2020, the World Business Council for Sustainable Development (WBCSD) set a target of net zero emissions by 2050 for all its members, including 200 of the world's largest corporations, with two years to comply.[49] Many of the top petrochemical, chemical, and plastics corporations are members of the WBCSD, including for example, BASF, Sabic, Sinopec, Borealis, and Covestro.

During a panel discussion at the World Petrochemical Conference held online in March 2021, several senior industry analysts reflected on their confidence about corporate pledges to meet the target of net zero emissions.[50] The panellists agreed that while the industry would make progress, it was unlikely that all of their specific targets would be met. However, they were aware that environmental regulations were changing quickly in response to the climate emergency, and one analyst cautioned that 'whether the specific targets are met, don't let that distract you from where we are going, where the world is going'. Another analyst concluded with a note of optimism, arguing that 'there is a younger generation of employees, investors, and consumers who are expecting the industry to be successful, maybe not in the timing and the exact targets, but the expectation is there. The industry needs to be successful in achieving these lower emissions goals that we have out there.' Tellingly, the theme of the World Petrochemical Conference in 2022 was decided: 'Navigating towards net zero'.

Much media attention has focused on the net zero pledges of oil majors and national governments, particularly with the Leaders' Summit on Climate in April 2021 hosted by the United States, featuring Joe

Biden's commitment to cut US emissions in half by 2030, and the UN Climate Conference (COP26) in Glasgow in November 2021.[51] Indeed, 'net zero' was a key buzzword throughout COP26, featuring in almost every presentation and announcement from governments and businesses.[52] On 'Finance Day', just after the World Leaders' Summit, Mark Carney, the former Governor of the Bank of England, unveiled the Glasgow Financial Alliance for Net Zero (GFANZ), including over $130 trillion of private capital commitments to net zero-aligned projects. To avoid greenwashing allegations, GFANZ would be backed by the formation of an International Sustainability Standards Board (ISSB) to create a global baseline for corporate sustainability disclosures using 'science-based targets'.[53] However, climate activists shot back that this indeed was 'pure greenwash', proclaiming that 'net zero is not zero' and running events that exposed the 'false climate solutions' of corporate and government net zero commitments, particularly their use of carbon offsetting.[54] According to campaigners from Global Witness, the fossil fuel industry had the largest delegation at the COP26, including more than 503 delegates who were associated with fossil fuel interests.[55] Not surprisingly, these delegates kept a low profile in the official programme: the oil majors were blocked from having a formal role in COP26 due to widespread doubts about their net zero plans.[56] The fossil fuel-dependent petrochemical industry was thus absent from COP26 discussions about decarbonizing 'hard-to-abate' heavy industries, which focused on steel and cement.

Despite the wide corporate take-up of net zero pledges, there has been less public scrutiny of the commitments of plastics industry players beyond the oil majors. Within the plastics value chain, the majority of net zero pledges have been concentrated on the producer end of the chain, including the vertically integrated oil and gas companies and multinational chemical companies, and on the consumer brand end of the chain, including consumer goods and beverage industries. While the oil and gas company pledges focus on increased spending on renewables and reductions in carbon intensity, the consumer brands redirect attention upstream along their supply chain. Coca-Cola, for instance, notes that 90% of the greenhouse gas emissions in its supply chain come from the activities of its suppliers, and thus its net zero action plan aims to support its suppliers at reducing emissions and increasing their use of renewable energy.[57] Similarly, Procter & Gamble has pledged to reduce its scope 1 emissions (direct emissions from sources owned or controlled by an organization) and scope 2 emissions (indirect emissions from energy use) through transitioning to renewable electricity and using nature-based carbon offsets, while excluding targets for scope 3 emissions (indirect emissions from sources that are not owned or controlled by an organization) because these are attributed to consumers.[58]

At the time of writing, the corporations in the middle of the chain, which make up the majority of the plastics sector, such as global packaging corporations Amcor, Novolex, and Berry Global, have been slow to join the rush to make net zero pledges, instead incorporating accredited low-carbon commitments into their circular economy strategies. For example, Amcor has introduced 'Reducing CO_2 Packaging' labels on its flexible packaging, one of several carbon labels that have been accredited by the UK-based company Carbon Trust.[59] Novolex refers to 'science-based targets' for limiting global warming to less than two degrees, in line with the Paris Agreement, in its 2020 sustainability report.[60] In April 2021, Berry Global announced that it was 'the first North American headquartered plastics packaging converter to have a 1.5 degree target validated by the Science-Based Target Initiative (SBTI) ... reinforcing the Company's commitment to a circular economy in alignment with the worldwide goal of a net-zero economy by 2050'.[61]

Many corporate proponents of the circular economy for plastics have responded to the net zero discourse by aligning the two concepts. In September 2019, the Ellen MacArthur Foundation released a report arguing that net zero targets could not be achieved without a circular economy, and that 45% of greenhouse gas emissions could be reduced by pursuing circularity.[62] This position has been echoed by other circular economy advocates, both in terms of strategic alignment with policy goals and in terms of practical outcomes, including the 45% headline figure.[63] The global waste management company Veolia released a report in 2021 which highlighted the importance of plastic recycling and the circular economy for achieving net zero targets. However, as we have seen in chapter 3, circular economy projects are not necessarily low-carbon, particularly in the case of plastics. One of the biggest problems with chemical recycling, the circular economy 'solution' to plastic waste, is that it is highly carbon-intensive. This poses a tremendous technical challenge for proposals to transform the petrochemical industry from using 99% virgin fossil fuel feedstocks to using 100% recycled or bio-feedstocks, as we will discuss in chapter 6.

Corporate pledges to achieve net zero emissions and to the circular economy share many points in common. They both represent coordinated industry responses to profound ecological crisis and involve voluntary aspirations rather than binding targets. Both rely on unproven technologies to get the difficult work done, including chemical recycling in the case of the circular economy and carbon sequestration in the case of net zero emissions. Both also rely heavily on energy efficiency measures to lower the emissions and waste from industrial processes. The added benefit of the two strategies, for industry, is that they mutually reinforce one another: the circular economy becomes the answer to net zero, and vice versa.

Poised for a Downturn?

The petrochemical and plastics industries have joined the race to net zero through incorporating it within the circular economy. So long as they can make everything circular and develop the appropriate technologies, using science-based targets, then they claim that their emissions can be reduced in line with net zero targets. The trouble is that industry leaders hold a monopoly on the expertise required to develop and scale up alternatives, and they are well-practised in co-opting and delaying regulations. While the petrochemical industry has been singled out as a key 'hard-to-abate' sector *and* faces increasing pressure to decarbonize, plastics are still seen as an exceptional use of fossil fuels for their 'essential' role in society. The role of plastics in fighting COVID-19 brought this role into sharp relief.

On the eve of the coronavirus pandemic, the climate emergency had become a major threat to business-as-usual for corporations along the plastics value chain. The oil industry has long relied on uncertainty campaigns and lobbying to delay climate action, while the petrochemical and plastics industries have claimed that plastics are actually, on balance, climate-friendly. However, these tactics could no longer stand up to criticism. The year 2019 witnessed a wave of climate divestment, costly climate litigation, and new investment requirements for corporations to declare climate risk. Investors publicly questioned the strategy of oil companies to invest in plastics markets, which would become stranded assets in the transition away from fossil fuels. The race to achieve global net zero emissions was on, and fossil fuel companies had come under pressure as never before. Or so it would seem. Corporations are always poised to turn a crisis into an opportunity.

At the beginning of 2020, the petrochemical industry was also preparing for a period of cyclical decline, but for different reasons. According to an industry expert, 2018 represented 'the sixth year of an extended upcycle in global chemical markets – characterized by robust demand, tight supply, and strong profitability. This extended period of profitability has caused a surge in reinvestment planning activity in North America, the Middle East, China and other Asia locations.'[64] However, by the end of 2019, the global expansion of petrochemical investments had led to overcapacity. The onset of the pandemic turned that situation around, to the benefit of many plastics producers.

5

Plastics in the Pandemic

There are only two reasons that the plastics industry will change, a polymer scientist once told me: war or legislation.[1] Corporations along the plastics value chain have faced a number of environmental and health crises, from toxic scandals to marine plastic waste and the climate emergency. Each of these crises has led to new laws and regulations, despite corporate efforts to undermine them. The petrochemical and plastics industries have also experienced deep economic shocks, including the 1973 oil crisis and the 2008 global financial crisis, in addition to major regional disruptions from oil spills, hurricanes, and other disasters. When the 1973 oil crisis first emerged, the *Modern Plastics* trade magazine editor Sidney Gross complained that the American plastics industry was 'facing more major crises than it has ever confronted before – all at once'.[2] These included 'supplies, flammability, toxicity, environment, and OSHA [Occupational Safety and Health Administration]'. However, Gross later wrote that the oil crisis was 'a very happy issue for us' because it enabled the industry to develop a new line of defence:

rather than wasting energy by using oil to make plastics, it was actually saving energy, by making lightweight materials that reduced the fuel costs of transportation.[3] Sound familiar?

The COVID-19 pandemic posed yet another kind of crisis for industry, again encompassing several major crises all at once. At first blush, the global health crisis seemed almost akin to war, presenting a new growth opportunity for industry to manufacture and serve new kinds of demand as part of the global fight against the virus. In the early months, analogies between the pandemic and war circulated widely in politics and the media, drawing on themes of national heroes, sacrifice, and the home front.[4] The petrochemical and plastics industries originated from literal wartime demand, and they relished their new 'essential' role in the metaphorical war against the invisible enemy. However, these analogies soon began to wear thin and drew criticisms of inward-looking nationalism, gradually receding as the pandemic progressed. Meanwhile, governments around the world began to focus on green recoveries, with many policymakers and investors starting to question the fossil fuel origins of plastics production.[5] In the long term, it may be that legislation will be the big game-changer.

Writing in the middle of the pandemic, which has changed through different waves, variants, vaccination rounds, and frontlines, it is too early to tell how the petrochemical and plastics industries will fare through the crisis. Instead, this chapter examines some of the dynamics of disruption, growth, and contestation for industry during the first eighteen months of the pandemic, concluding with some reflections on the prospects for more far-reaching plastics legislation. Importantly, this chapter resists the temptation to characterize industry as being in control of unpredictable disruptive events. The remarkable growth in demand for single-use plastics due to the health crisis came as a surprise even for industry experts. From a policy perspective, it is important to recognize that the future exponential growth of plastics is far from inevitable, particularly in the context of the race to reach net zero carbon emissions.

As many researchers and activists have observed, the petrochemical and plastics industries acted quickly at the beginning of the pandemic to position their products as 'essential', lobbying to reverse single-use plastics bans and to delay circular economy initiatives.[6] However, these efforts met with mixed success, both in terms of changing public perceptions of plastics, and in terms of setting back regulations. Although there have been many delays and reversals of single-use plastics bans during the pandemic, there have also been moves towards stronger environmental regulations. By the spring of 2021, several industry experts were optimistic about the future of plastics beyond the pandemic, but some were more cautious.[7] As one industry analyst forewarned, 'Since the environmental movement emerged in the 1960s, it has been a one-way street towards stricter regulations.'[8] Despite the importance of plastics for tackling the health crisis, the wider implications of the pandemic for the future of the plastics industry are far from settled.

Weathering the Storm

In the two years leading up to the pandemic, the public backlash against plastic was a major concern for industry leaders. As a corporate executive remarked during an industry event early in 2019: 'We need to get the image of plastic in oceans out of the public's mind. Otherwise, we could lose our social licence to operate.'[9] Of course, the pandemic did not take the image of plastic in oceans out of the public's mind. However, it did highlight in a very real and urgent way the importance of many plastic products for health care and hygiene. At the virtual World Petrochemical Conference in April 2020, an industry analyst commented on this unexpected shift: 'Ironically, sustainability, the issue that was dominating the conversation until just a few weeks ago, seems to be fading into the background, at least for the moment. And polyethylene may even be gaining some public favour as it plays a high-profile role in combating the greatest health risk to our planet in modern history.'[10]

As crude oil plummeted to historical lows in April 2020 and much of the global economy ground to a halt, industry analysts warned of flattening plastics growth and evaporating profit margins.[11] However, their predictions of economic collapse were premature. Plastics proved essential in the global fight against the virus, used in medical devices, personal protective equipment, and packaging food and medical supplies. One year later, an industry analyst marvelled at the virtual World Petrochemical Conference:

> This time last year we felt that the global industry was on the verge of a downturn, and that this downturn would be driven by excess capacity additions that would frankly last through 2023. Clearly this has not happened. Instead we've seen polyethylene producers flourish in ways that no one would have anticipated. We did see the beginnings of a downturn in late 2019, but COVID ended up being a demand driver. We saw consumer buying habits change, we saw work-from-home culture develop, e-commerce surged, and much of this new demand that we saw appears to represent a sustainable increase in demand.[12]

By 'sustainable', naturally, the analyst did not mean that the new plastics demand was good for the environment. He meant that the demand for the most commonly used plastic worldwide, polyethylene, found in flexible packaging, would continue to rise beyond the pandemic. While demand for health care products would eventually fall, he predicted, changing consumer habits and work-from-home cultures would be here to stay.

Other industry analysts reported similar windfalls, with unexpectedly high demand for polypropylene, used in face masks and takeaway containers, and for PET, used in beverage bottles and food packaging. Exceptionally, in the middle of a global recession, these plastics had achieved net positive growth in 2020, above even 2019 levels.[13] Durable plastic end markets, by contrast, for example in furniture, automobiles, appliances, and construction, saw declining growth in 2020.[14] The pandemic also delayed several million tons of new petrochemical capacity starts, preventing a cyclical downturn that had been anticipated due to overcapacity. 'All things considered, the industry weathered the storm remarkably well, with relatively resilient volumes and profits,'[15] remarked the authors of a McKinsey report in May 2021 on the impacts of COVID-19 on the petrochemical industry. As another industry consultant explained, a number of factors had come together in 2020 – which included not only COVID-19, but also the relaxation of trade war tariffs between the United States and China, and extreme weather disruptions (hurricanes and freezing weather in Texas) – to make 'a perfect storm turning a crisis into an opportunity for polyolefins [the largest group of plastics polymers, comprising polyethylene and polypropylene]'.[16]

The pandemic vindicated long-held industry claims about the benefits of plastics for society, at least in the case of health care and sanitary products. This temporary respite from public anti-plastic sentiment opened the door for industry to push back against single-use plastics bans. However, the importance of plastics for fighting the coronavirus did not change the minds of environmental and anti-plastic activists, who were keeping close tabs on industry movements.[17] In March 2020, the Plastics Association (PLASTICS) wrote a letter to the US Department of Health and Human Services requesting that they make a public statement about the health and safety benefits of using single-use plastics, as the 'sanitary choice'.[18] Later that month, Greenpeace issued a research brief about how the plastics industry had manipulated the media with misleading scientific claims about the 'sanitary' benefits of plastics over reusables, citing the PLASTICS letter, in order to reverse single-use plastic bag policies.[19] The brief claimed that the industry had deflected attention from a peer-reviewed study that COVID-19 could survive on plastic surfaces for up to three days, longer than most other materials, including cardboard. Ironically, the authors said, the industry had relied on this very study to promote the use of single-use plastic bags, by conflating it with older industry-funded studies showing that bacteria can be transmitted on reusable bags.[20]

The next month, Break Free From Plastic activists sent an open letter to the European Commission citing the false health messages of the plastics industry, including the aggressive tactics of the US industry-led initiative 'Bag the Ban', and another industry lobbying letter, this time from the European Plastics Converters (EuPC) to the European Commission asking for the postponement of the Single-Use Plastics Directive, legislation introduced in June 2019 banning single-use plastics starting in 2021 and placing more responsibility on plastics producers for the disposal of post-consumer waste.[21] 'COVID-19 is a mirror and magnifier of our existing problems,' the Break Free From Plastic activists wrote, pointing to the unjust health consequences of toxic plastics production in petrochemical communities, and to the increased exposure to the virus for waste management workers and communities in the global South.[22]

The European Commission rejected the industry's request to delay the EU Directive on Single-Use Plastics. However, multiple single-use plastics bans and deposit return schemes were reversed or delayed in countries around the world, across North America, Europe, Africa, and Asia.[23] These policy setbacks were due in part to effective industry lobbying, but also to the challenges of protecting the public and delivery and waste management workers from exposure to COVID-19. Many recycling centres closed because of the low cost of virgin plastics after the crude oil crash, combined with safety concerns about managing hazardous waste. In June 2020, 115 public health experts from 18 countries signed a statement published by Greenpeace and UPSTREAM (members of the Break Free From Plastics movement) that reusable bags and containers were safe to use, provided that basic hygiene measures were observed.[24] As the first wave of the pandemic subsided, however, a number of the single-use plastics bans that had been retracted or delayed were reinstated.[25]

During the first wave of lockdowns, a raft of media stories about the 'plastic pandemic' swept in, drawing attention to the implications of the health crisis for the plastic one.[26] Stories spotlighted problems with this plastic resurgence, from the tons of hazardous personal protective equipment entering into waste streams, to the enormous volumes of packaging waste from online shopping deliveries, to the circular economy recycling programmes that had stalled. The *New York Times* published a scathing exposé of industry lobbying to limit Kenya's restrictions on single-use plastics and plastic waste imports, which the American Chemistry Council swiftly denied.[27] Other media reports revealed that oil and petrochemical companies had received enormous bailouts in the aftermath of the crude oil crash.[28]

Plastics during the pandemic did gain *some* public favour, restored to their original paradoxical status as both a miracle and a menace for society. As far as industry was concerned, this was enough: it had regained its social licence to operate. By the end of 2020, industry leaders had fully embraced the new pandemic narrative about the essential role of plastics in society and many expressed optimism about their future growth. At the virtual World Petrochemical Conference in March 2021, industry analysts identified four key 'COVID demand drivers': food packaging, bag ban delays, online shopping, and hygiene and medical. Only one of these drivers directly related to fighting the virus, while the others were indirectly related, serving the consumer demands of billions of people under various forms of lockdown. Notably, China was a major consumer growth market, with a 31% rise in express parcel deliveries and a 25% rise in online food deliveries, and forecasts for future demand growth across the industry depended heavily on plastics markets in the country. As one petrochemical industry executive enthused:

The COVID-19 pandemic highlighted how essential all our products are to everyone in society around the globe. We saw record sales and record volumes for our products throughout the pandemic, but we had to shift constantly to the changing demand patterns. … In spite of the COVID pandemic, over the long term we can continue to see that kind of growth, and we're going to see that accelerate as economies reopen around the world, we're starting to see signs of that today. All of this is really driven by the world's growing global middle class, and that's going to drive demand for the products that we produce. COVID-19 didn't change our long-term view on the fundamentals.[29]

Gone were the hand-wringing accounts about how to win back the public. Sustainability and the circular economy were still agenda items, but industry representatives discussed these topics in a nonchalant manner, making breezy comments such as: 'Plastics are a sustainable solution to many alternatives, but we need to ensure we have proper disposal and circular options when these materials come to the end of their useful life'; and: 'Across the industry chemical recycling is solvable, we just need to get on with it.'[30] The main existential threat that the industry was facing was pressure from investors to integrate ESG criteria into their investment decisions, but for now this was hitting energy markets rather than plastics. Once again, plastics were the exception, the driver of growth – and it was all down to middle-class consumption.

Hearing these glowing industry reports about single-use plastics growth, I couldn't help feeling guilty about the plastics that have entered my home in the United Kingdom during the pandemic. Many environmental activists and scholars have pointed out that one of the key tactics of industry is to blame the consumer for plastic waste, which diverts attention from corporate responsibility.[31] The plastics crisis is a systemic problem, however, and most people are locked into supply chains and infrastructures, unable to simply opt out of plastics consumption. More specifically, the sociologists Olivier Coutard and Elizabeth Shove have observed that consumption within large infrastructural systems is 'an outcome of complex demand-making and recip-rocal influence between supply and demand', based on strategies of 'predict and provide – in which planners anticipate future "need" and build capacity capable of meeting it – [which] have acted as self-fulfilling prophecies: generating the very forms of demand to which investments and infrastructures are allegedly a response'.[32] That being said, consumption is also highly unequal. According to a recent study published in the journal *Science Advances*, the United Kingdom is second only to the United States in terms of the amount of plastic waste generated per person, at 99 kg and 109 kg per person per year, respectively, and supermarkets with overpackaged food are one of the main problems.[33] By contrast, the global average of plastics consumption is 45 kg per person per year, and as little as 4 kg per person per year in India.[34] Looking at the consequences of one's own actions, from a privileged standpoint, multiplied and intensified across the planet, invites a kind of vertigo.

Ballooning Plastic Facts

Plastic products have offered essential medical and hygiene protection for billions of people around the world during the pandemic, and takeaway containers and e-commerce deliveries have been a lifeline for struggling businesses. The irony is that the increased demand for single-use plastics due to health and safety concerns has led to rising volumes of hazardous waste, posing a threat to public health due to potential virus transmission in addition to toxicity concerns.[35] Enormous quantities of medical plastic waste have been generated during the pandemic, including an estimated 129 billion face masks and 65 billion gloves used globally every month in the first year.[36] In addition to medical waste, a great deal of household recycling waste was classified as hazardous and thus incinerated or sent to landfill, leading to higher releases of greenhouse gases and toxic substances through burning or 'leakage' into the natural environment.[37] Millions of informal waste pickers around the world, from Southeast Asia to Africa to South America, have faced multiple risks during the pandemic, including exposures to contaminated materials, losing their means of survival due to lockdown restrictions and scrapyard closures, and, in some cases, police reprisals for leaving their homes to collect plastic products.[38]

As the pandemic has unfolded, the number of facts about plastics has ballooned. Hundreds of research articles and reports have emerged; some speculative, with doomsday predictions of being inundated with waste, others meticulously cataloguing the damages: the volumes of face masks accumulating in cities and oceans; the litany of corporate lobbying tactics; the number of regulatory rollbacks; the constantly rising figures of plastics production and pollution; the open burning of plastic waste near to vulnerable workers; and the relationship between accumulating plastic waste, urban flooding, and the spread of zoonotic diseases (infectious diseases that spread from non-human animals to humans).[39] Some have hard-hitting messages, such as Greenpeace's 2021 report *Trashed*, about the United Kingdom's dumping of plastic waste in Turkey.[40] Others have pointed to unexpected turns of event, such as an article published in December 2020 puzzling over the relative lack of pandemic-related waste in Africa.[41]

It is difficult to make sense of these disjointed flows of information, mediated through the Web, interspersed with other alarming global news. The current analyses and predictions quickly become displaced with the latest twists and turns.[42] In *Being Ecological*, the philosopher Timothy Morton argues that most forms of ecological writing involve an information dump of facts, which can be disorienting and unproductive. Morton's answer is to avoid facts altogether, especially what he calls 'factoids', devoid of interpretation.[43] On the one hand, I disagree with such a flippant assessment, especially given all the attacks on science in the post-truth age. Facts are impossible to avoid, and they are important when put in the context of wider arguments. On the other hand,

Morton's intervention has some resonance in pandemic times, where the bad news cycle is relentless. In the rest of this chapter, I will try to avoid the exhaustion of the information dump, though not to the point of avoiding facts. Instead, I will now focus on some consistent criticisms of the top corporate polluters that have emerged through the pandemic, which have highlighted the obvious problems with corporate voluntary commitments, before discussing the prospects for more binding regulations through green recoveries.

Top Polluters

While voluntary corporate commitments to end plastic waste have flooded in, the plastics crisis has kept getting worse. Corporations have increasingly come under scrutiny from environmental activists and organizations for their failure to stop polluting. Some of most scathing reports have emerged during the pandemic, such as the Changing Markets Foundation's report *Talking Trash*, which concluded that '[t]he Covid-19 health crisis has, once again, shown that Big Plastic is always primed and ready to co-opt a crisis to their advantage, pushing to undermine environmental legislation or any restrictions on their products. ... [T]he plastics industry does not have people's best interests at heart; instead, it is making cold calculations to carry on with business as usual.'[44] The *Talking Trash* report focused on the inadequate voluntary commitments of the top plastics polluters in the consumer goods and beverage industries, and the corporate 'playbook' for undermining plastics legislation, particularly deposit return schemes and single-use plastics bans.

One of the key targets of environmental organizations has been the top corporate polluters. In 2020, for the third year in a row, Break Free From Plastic named Coca-Cola, PepsiCo, and Nestlé as the top plastic polluters in their annual Branch Audit, based on the collection of thousands of pieces of branded plastic trash from 15,000 volunteers.[45] Coca-Cola was ranked first on the list, which produces by far the most plastic packaging in the world, 2.9 million metric tonnes per year. The non-profit Tearfund reached similar conclusions in its March 2020 report, *The Burning Question*, which singled out Coca-Cola, PepsiCo, Nestlé, and Unilever as the biggest plastic polluters in six countries: China, India, the Philippines, Brazil, Mexico, and Nigeria.[46] The Tearfund report found that plastics companies were responsible for flooding these countries with billions of single-use packaging products, despite knowing that these countries have ineffective waste management systems. Another report released in May 2021 by the Minderloo Foundation, *The Plastic Waste Makers Index*, focused attention on the plastics producers, revealing that twenty firms produce 55% of the world's single-use plastic waste.[47] This list of the top twenty firms includes the largest plastics producers (i.e., major petrochemical companies), with the oil major ExxonMobil as the frontrunner, followed by the multi-national chemical company Dow, and then the Chinese state-owned oil and gas company Sinopec.

Several of the top plastics producers (petrochemical companies) and consumer brands (beverage and consumer goods companies) have been singled out as the top polluters. The packaging converters have gone less noticed – although major packaging companies such as Novolex have taken some heat for their role in the industry's campaign to reverse plastic bag bans early in the pandemic.[48] However, the problem of unlimited plastics growth is so much bigger than just the plastics corporations. Virtually every modern industry relies on plastics in some shape or form. Take Amazon, for example, another business success story of the pandemic. According to a report from the non-profit ocean advocacy group Oceana, Amazon was responsible for 485 million pounds of packaging waste in 2019, a volume that would have increased in 2020 along with the 38% growth in sales.[49]

For all of the naming and shaming, you might think that the roll call of top corporate plastics polluters has had little effect. The big reveal that the biggest plastics producers, brands, and retailers are also the biggest polluters comes as no surprise. Moreover, the allegation that corporations make weak voluntary commitments has no legal repercussions, at least not yet, in the absence of more binding regulations. Corporations are used to claims about greenwashing. At an industry event back in March 2019, a petrochemical executive read out a quote from Greenpeace that labelled the Alliance to End Plastic Waste a 'desperate attempt by corporate polluters', after which the corporate audience laughed.[50] An Alliance CEO responded calmly to this allegation that they had expected claims of greenwashing but emphasized that the Alliance really was a step forward in terms of collaboration, innovation, and ambition. This shows the power of wilful ignorance. Yet throughout the pandemic, the top polluter roll call has in fact had an important effect, countering corporate narratives about the 'sanitary' benefits of all single-use plastics, emphasizing the fundamental problem with corporate voluntary commitments, and contributing to policy debates about the urgent need for binding regulations.

Beyond NGOs, many organizations have started to realize that voluntary corporate commitments will be not enough to stop the plastics crisis. The July 2020 report *Breaking the Plastic Wave* by the Pew Charitable Trusts and SYSTEMIQ Ltd found that even if government and industry honour their latest voluntary commitments to the circular economy, they are likely to reduce annual plastic leakage into the ocean by only 7% relative to 'Business-as-Usual' (whereby the amount of plastic waste in oceans will nearly triple from current levels by 2040, from 11 million to 29 million metric tonnes per year). This anticipated increase in plastic waste is directly connected to plastics production, which is expected to double by 2040. According to the report, the surge in plastics production will be driven by four compounding factors: population growth; rising per capita plastic use; increased consumption of non-recyclable materials; and 'the growing share of plastic consumption occurring in countries with low rates of collection'.[51] With endorsements from anti-plastic activists and corporate stakeholders alike, the report stresses the need for more coordinated and ambitious action, beyond existing commitments. This is an important step in trying to overcome the political impasse between different stake-holders. Supported by the Ellen MacArthur Foundation, the report echoes themes of the New Plastics Economy Global Commitment, which points to the need to move beyond recycling and voluntary commitments to address the plastics waste crisis on a more systemic level. However, the Pew Charitable Trusts and SYSTEMIQ still frame the issue in terms of resolving the problem of too much 'leakage'. Rising plastics production is taken as an inevitable force. What is more, the gloomy predictions of the *Breaking the Plastic Wave* report, which was released in the first year of the pandemic, do not even factor in the unanticipated burst in global demand for single-use plastics.

The Regulatory Front of Green Recoveries

One important lever for changing the plastics industry has gained traction during the pandemic: the dawning realization by many investors and policymakers that green recovery paths to net zero will need to phase out fossil fuels altogether, including virgin plastics. In September 2020, as noted in chapter 4, the think tank Carbon Tracker warned investors in plastics about the risk of having stranded assets in the transition away from fossil fuels.[52] Plastics is the last pillar of oil demand growth, its researchers argued, but this pillar would be removed very soon by increasing regulatory and recycling pressures, accelerated by green recovery packages. The *Plastic Waste Makers Index* also makes this point very clearly, calling out the leading plastics producers for continuing to rely on virgin plastics feedstocks, as well as the major investors and banks that have 'enabled the single-use plastics crisis' through investing billions of dollars in virgin plastics production.[53]

The need to reduce the reliance of plastics on fossil fuels has also featured in a number of policy proposals for addressing the plastics crisis, dovetailing with the momentum to respond to the climate emergency through green recoveries after the pandemic. The US Break Free From Plastic Bill re-emerged early in 2021 under the Biden presidency, incorporating calls from environmental activists and frontline communities to halt petrochemical projects and to hold corporations accountable for waste and emissions throughout the plastic lifecycle. Plastics sustainability, incorporating net zero emissions targets, is also a prominent part of the European Green Deal. Furthermore, reducing virgin plastics production is a core (if contested) topic for discussions about the need for a new UN treaty on plastics, amid growing recognition from many governments, organizations, and researchers that the problem of plastic pollution extends through the plastics lifecycle, from the extraction of raw materials through to manufacturing, consumption, waste, and pollution.[54]

If there is any insight that can be gained from looking at the ways that corporations have responded to the plastics crisis, which has magnified during the pandemic, it is the power of legislation. Binding laws and regulations offer less room for manoeuvre than voluntary commitments, especially when it comes to bans. The plastics industry is more concerned about the threat of the European Single-Use Plastics Directive, which is binding legislation, than the Ellen MacArthur New Plastics Economy Global Commitment, which is based on voluntary circular economy commitments. Outright bans of specific plastic products, on the grounds of protecting the environment or public health, effectively take these products off the market. Despite the delays to single-use plastics bans during the pandemic, there are a number of bans on plastic bags, straws, microbeads, and other single-use plastic products in countries around the world. Throughout the history of the plastics industry, there have also been a number of bans related to toxicity concerns, including vinyl aerosol products, BPA in toys and baby bottles, and polystyrene food containers, amongst others. In the near future, as the climate emergency worsens, there may also be bans on virgin plastics.

While legislation is an important tool for reining in corporate excess, the petrochemical and plastics industries have demonstrated time after time that they will fight to delay and undermine this. Corporations will also find ways of working around the rules, for example through loopholes, such as those in the Basel Convention, which enable the continuation of unequal international shipments of hazardous plastic waste through 'prior informed consent', and offering opportunities for corporations to profit from marketing risky technological solutions to vulnerable communities that are burdened with waste.[55] In the absence of legislative bans, corporations have continued to produce products that are known to be hazardous to health and the environment, and to wage legal and publicity battles to be able to do so.

In the long term, according to industry forecasts, the biggest threat to petrochemical and plastics markets beyond the pandemic will be how quickly investment shifts in response to regulatory pressures to address ESG issues, particularly in the race to net zero. As one analyst put it, 'What we're going to see is real movement on the policy and regulatory front. The question is how quickly that will move in line with investments.'[56] With the success of single-use plastics during the first year of the pandemic, they didn't see this as an immediate threat for plastics markets, but they were watching this space very closely.

In order to address the plastics crisis, the pandemic has made clear that we need legislation and binding regulations, but we also need another lever of change. I don't mean war, as the polymer scientist quipped, although of course it is important to keep up the pressure on the top corporate polluters and virgin plastics producers, stay vigilant against regulatory pushback, and continue to struggle for just and sustainable alternatives. What I mean is more basic: questioning the dominant assumption that there can be continual plastics growth on a finite planet. If this assumption could be overturned, aligning with the growing consensus that the world needs to transition away from fossil fuels, then that would be a starting point for meaningful change.

6

How Can We Curb
the Plastics Crisis?

There is an obvious way to curb the global plastics crisis:
'turn off the tap', as many environmental activists and
scholars have insisted.[1] Stop producing and consuming
so much plastic. This is not as simple as it sounds.
The 'let's be realistic' narrative of the plastics industry
comes into play whenever solutions to the plastics crisis
are proposed. Generally speaking, the more a proposal
disrupts the possibilities for endless plastics growth,
the less realistic it is perceived to be by political and
economic elites. Yet if we want to be realistic about
plastics, on a planetary level of multi-species survival,
then we must recognize the urgency of stopping their
unsustainable growth.

Given this political impasse, how can we address the
question of what to do? It is not that there is a shortage
of practical solutions to the plastics crisis. Every report
filled with plastic facts ends with the question of what
to do. Most of the solutions are familiar: reduce, reuse,
and recycle; prevent 'leakage' through responsible waste
management; and 'decouple' fossil fuel extraction from
plastics to make it all circular. The more contentious

issues are whether to focus more on reduction, reuse, recycling, or other 'Rs' of the circular economy, and what kinds of legislation and regulation will be most effective. The problem is that despite all the solutions, plastics markets keep growing, and the plastics crisis keeps getting worse.

There is a widening gap between the severity of the plastics crisis and the possibility that we can overcome the problem if only we find the right solutions and work together. In fact, the idea that humanity under capitalism can provide the solutions to ecological problems is one of the most prevailing modern myths. It is the happy ending most people want to hear. I do want to be optimistic, too, but it's difficult to muster. In this chapter, I will reflect on some of the practical possibilities for curbing the plastics crisis that I think could be the most promising.

A Paris Agreement for Plastics

Over the past few years, there have been increasing calls for a 'Paris Agreement for plastics', in recognition of the fact that the global plastics crisis is intensifying at an unprecedented rate, similar to out-of-control global heating.[2] Nearly 150 countries have some form of legislation to phase out single-use plastics, and there are several international and regional agreements related to marine pollution and the plastic waste trade. However, the global governance of plastics to date remains fragmented, uncoordinated, and uneven.[3] In July 2020, environmental scientists published a review of international regulations on plastic pollution and concluded that 'it is not clear what the benefits – if any – of the multitude of norms, regulations, laws and recommendations that have been proposed and/or implemented in recent years are'.[4]

The idea of a binding global treaty on plastic pollution has drawn support from governments, business groups, and environmental activists alike, as a common framework for catalysing, coordinating, and standardizing international efforts to address the plastics crisis. At the fourth session of the United Nations Environment Assembly (UNEA) in March 2019, a number of member states supported the development of a binding UN treaty for plastics.[5] In May 2019, the first 'activist-to-industry' ocean plastics summit was held aboard a ship in the Atlantic Garbage Patch, including 165 representatives from plastics corporations, environmental NGOs, and informal waste pickers.[6] They formed the Ocean Plastics Leadership Network to help accelerate a 'Paris Agreement for plastics', a significant move towards overcoming long-standing differences between corporations and civil society. In *The Business Case for a UN Treaty on Plastic Pollution*, published in 2020 by the World Wildlife Fund, the Ellen MacArthur Foundation, and Boston Consulting Group, business supporters of a global plastics treaty argued that it would create a level playing field across the plastics value chain. Echoing other industry forewarnings, they advised: 'It is no longer a question of whether regulation is coming, but what regulation is coming.'[7]

As this book goes to print, negotiations to create a global treaty on plastic pollution are expected to commence at the fifth UNEA in February 2022, following a preparatory hybrid Ministerial Conference in September 2021. More than 100 countries are in favour of a binding treaty.[8] However, negotiating such a complex global agreement involving competing political and economic interests, which will take several years to negotiate and enter into force, will present considerable challenges.[9] Member states that support the treaty agree on the need for activities in environmental monitoring and reporting, preventing plastic pollution, coordination with other international and regional laws and regulations, and providing technical support to policymakers and financial support for developing countries.[10] A more controversial issue, however, is the question of limiting production. Many environmental activists insist that the treaty should include an objective to cap and reduce the amount of overall virgin plastics production. By contrast, corporations would like to keep the scope of the treaty focused on reducing plastic waste. Given the interests at stake, environmental advocates of the treaty expect strong lobbying from industry. According to David Azoulay, manager of CIEL in Geneva, 'The biggest form of lobbying from the plastic industry is trying to frame the narrative. They claim that plastic is not a problem until it becomes waste and is littered in the environment. They're not the ones responsible, consumers are.'[11]

Not everyone agrees that a Paris Agreement for plastics would be the best way of addressing the crisis. In a policy brief for the International Institute for Sustainable Development, Tallash Kantai argues that there could be both advantages and disadvantages to such a treaty. If it ends up avoiding the question of production, Kantai argues, then 'addressing plastic only when it becomes waste could leave the world in a never-ending waste cycle'.[12] I agree that this is a risk, but at the same time, the world is already well along the path towards a never-ending waste cycle. By working towards a global treaty dedicated to plastic pollution, at least there would be a basis for future dialogue, research, and action to try to change course. It is worth observing that the original Paris Agreement is but one step in global efforts to address the climate emergency, not the end goal, and it has many flaws. Still, it is an important step.

The 'Paris Agreement for plastics' framing of a global treaty is also apt, implicitly aligning the plastics crisis with the climate crisis. On the one hand, this framing seeks to elevate the plastics crisis to the same level of planetary threat, but on the other hand, it underscores the gap between the two crises in terms of global governance. The climate emergency is widely recognized as the greatest environmental threat of our times, while other ecological crises, including the plastics crisis, tend to be subsumed within it. Given the global momentum behind addressing the climate crisis, drawing connections between plastics and climate could be a strong lever for further action. Recently, biologist Susan Shaw has argued that plastic is 'the evil twin of climate change', pointing out the links between oil and gas production and low-cost plastic manufacturing.[13] This resonates with the warning from environmental health leader Theo Colborn that 'we've got to make the fossil fuel connection' between oil and gas extraction and toxic petrochemicals, particularly in the case of fracking.[14]

Reducing plastics needs to be seen as part of the necessary green transition away from fossil fuels, as opposed to expanding plastics as a hedge against it, as corporations are doing. Yet at the same time, exponential plastics growth needs to be seen as an existential threat in itself. What this would mean in practice for an effective binding treaty on plastic pollution would be a tangible commitment to limiting plastics growth.

Ironically, one of the most effective ways of highlighting the need to limit plastics production rather than only addressing plastic waste could be through focusing even more closely on the problem of waste. Although a global treaty on plastic pollution would be unlikely to resolve entrenched problems of waste colonialism, it could provide a new framework to address the unequal hazardous plastic waste trade, especially with the support of Break Free From Plastic activists, NGOs, and political leaders from countries in Africa, Southeast Asia, and other regions that are disproportionately burdened with waste. One of the key priorities for a proposed global plastics treaty is to provide financial resources for better waste management systems and for the remediation of existing waste in countries that are burdened with waste.[15] Another is to coordinate and strengthen efforts to address plastic pollution across existing agreements, including the Basel Convention, and to improve standards, monitoring, and accountability measures. This would be a positive move, but only a start.

While the United Nations has been criticized by many scholars for reproducing colonial power structures, issues of global environmental justice and environmental racism have started to enter mainstream UN policy debates.[16] In March 2021, UN experts called 'Cancer Alley' in Louisiana a 'serious and disproportionate' example of environmental racism and raised human rights concerns about planned petrochemical developments in the area's St James Parish, a predominantly Black community that already has a high concentration of petrochemical plants.[17] UNEP and the environmental justice NGO Azul also co-published a report in 2021 highlighting the 'neglected' global attention to environmental justice impacts of plastic pollution, which disproportionately burden low-income communities and communities of colour across the plastics lifecycle.[18] Of course, the environmental justice impacts of plastic pollution have not been 'neglected' by the many frontline and fenceline communities around the world that have struggled against unjust toxic exposures to petrochemical pollution, waste incineration, and dumping. Geographer Thom Davies makes a related point in an article about everyday experiences of petrochemical pollution in 'Cancer Alley'. Reflecting on English professor Rob Nixon's widely cited description of the slow violence of pollution as 'a violence that occurs gradually and out of sight, a violence of delayed destruction that is dispersed across time and space',[19] Davies asks the question: 'Out of sight to whom?'[20] For decades, the experiences and knowledge claims of people who live with toxic pollution have been systemically discounted by governments and corporations.

The continual production of disposable plastics is made possible by the ability of people to send their waste elsewhere, to landfills, incinerators, and recycling units. As we noted in chapter 3, this is what Max Liboiron calls waste colonialism: assuming access to Land as a sink.[21] So long as waste is taken away, out of sight and smell, from kerbsides and residential areas, plastic waste will remain an abstract problem for many people, out there in the ocean, on the edges of cities, in different neighbourhoods, or in faraway countries. In some cases, raising public awareness about the unjust hazards of plastic pollution can have a significant impact on legislation. For example, as we also saw in chapter 3, the Chinese government's decision to ban plastic waste imports was influenced by international and national public reactions to the 2016 documentary *Plastic China*, which showed the toxic conditions of everyday life for families who depended on a small recycling factory out of necessity.[22] When China imposed its ban on imported plastic waste in 2018, the unequal global trade in post-consumer plastic waste came into the international spotlight. The amendment to the Basel Convention in 2019 to reclassify contaminated plastic scrap as hazardous waste was an important step towards regulating the international waste trade and empowering countries to refuse unwanted waste. However, it has not prevented plastic waste colonialism.[23] Where politics, money, and colonial ideologies are involved, unwanted waste has a way of finding new destinations.

In short, it is impossible to stem the tide of plastic waste without limiting plastics production. Yet the continual growth of plastics production cannot be sustained without generating enormous volumes of plastic waste. If we fail to recognize this destructive relationship, and continue to frame waste as 'leakage' that just needs to be better managed through the circular economy, meaningful systemic change will never be achieved. However, the problem with waste colonialism is that it is not only material, but also ideological, deeply embedded in dominant worldviews – which takes us to the corporations that are responsible for plastic pollution.

Holding Corporations Accountable

What can we reasonably expect corporations to do to address the escalating plastics crisis? Limiting toxic and unsustainable plastics growth is against their profit-seeking interests. As this book has shown, corporations across the plastics value chain have fought to maintain markets that they know are harmful to health, including vinyl aerosol products, food packaging that leaches BPA, and cookware with PFAS chemicals, to name just a few. They have aggressively marketed billions of consumer goods in non-recyclable single-use plastic sachets to countries in Southeast Asia and Africa, while knowing that these countries have problems with waste management. Through powerful industry associations, corporations have lobbied against single-use plastics bans and other plastics legislation, and funded studies to show the climate and health benefits of their products. They have also taken a proactive role in responding to sustainability pressures, by seeking to co-opt the circular economy agenda, advocating recycling above all other solutions, and directing blame towards individual consumers and mismanaged waste. Just as the world seemed to be turning against plastics, the pandemic highlighted in stark and unprecedented ways how plastics are important for the large-scale management of health crises, as the cheapest and most scalable material on hand, given their embedded infrastructures.

The point is that corporations do not and will not voluntarily limit their own markets, even if there is a compelling case to do so in order to protect health or the environment. Voluntary corporate-led initiatives will never be sufficient to address the social and ecological consequences of the plastics crisis. This is not to say that it couldn't be otherwise, that the twenty-first-century new corporation's ethos of 'doing well by doing good' could not be pushed further into different laws or cultures of capitalism.[24] In fact, the rapid shift by global investors towards using ESG metrics has provided a new boost to this ethos during the pandemic, with corporate leaders discussing the need to shift from 'value-to-values' and address three new Rs: risk, regulation, and returns.[25] The economist Mariana Mazzucato has argued persuasively that there is a key difference between value creation and value destruction in the global economy, and that corporations should not be rewarded for destructive and extractive practices.[26] However, under the prevailing growth-driven norms of global capitalism, and given the track record of plastics corporations to date, it seems unlikely that they will give up on unsustainable markets without compulsion. Plastics markets need to be limited through binding legislation, regulations, and social sanctions (e.g., reputational damage). These restrictions will require continual monitoring and enforcement through strong accountability measures.

Beyond bans, many governments have introduced EPR legislation to hold corporations responsible for the full lifecycle of their products. EPR is effectively an extension of the 'polluter pays' principle, where the producers of pollution have to pay for the costs of damages to the environment. The Organization for Economic Cooperation and Development (OECD) defines EPR as a 'policy approach under which producers are given a significant responsibility – financial and/or physical – for the treatment or disposal of post-consumer products', including take-back schemes, recycling, and final disposal.[27] In principle, EPR would incentivize producers not only to improve recycling systems but also to reduce waste generation at the source through designing products with increased recyclability and durability. However, a number of studies have shown that EPR policies have thus far had little influence in persuading producers to adopt eco-design practices.[28]

The first EPR legislation was introduced for packaging in Germany in 1992, and it has been a key part of European policy since the early 2000s.[29] A number of US states have also introduced such legislation, and Canada has had a national EPR strategy since 2009, although only some provinces have implemented EPR policies for packaging.[30] In practice, EPR policies in different national and regional contexts are highly fragmented and inconsistent, given the complexities of plastic supply chains, flexible approaches for implementing EPR requirements, and limited accountability measures.[31] Plastics producers typically meet their EPR responsibilities through paying intermediaries for collection and waste management. Some environmentalists argue that mandatory deposit return schemes are one of the most effective EPR policies, as they result in higher rates of collection than kerbside recycling, but many beverage corporations have opposed these schemes because of the costs.[32]

Many researchers have criticized EPR policies for failing to address waste prevention at the source, and for a lack of a common approach.[33] Some advocates for a global plastics treaty have called for a global EPR scheme in order to address the challenges of plastic products across complex global supply chains.[34] Such a scheme would involve the development of global design standards and the provision of waste management assistance to countries to regulate the plastic products placed on their market, with the aim of harmonizing global markets and simplifying regulatory processes for industry. Furthermore, there has been a push in both Europe and the United States to strengthen EPR legislation. In 2018, the European Union introduced EPR legislation mandating that all producers pay for separate waste collection in Europe by 2025, as part of its Circular Economy Action Plan.[35] The European Green Deal, which was unveiled in December 2019, includes a 'sustainable products' policy to promote the reduction and reuse of materials before recycling them.[36]

Echoing EU legislation, the US Break Free From Plastic Pollution Act, first proposed (and rejected) in 2020 and reintroduced in 2021 under the Biden Administration, proposes single-use plastics bans and a nationwide deposit return scheme.[37] It also goes further, proposing a three-year moratorium on new plastic refineries and explicitly addressing issues of environmental justice for frontline and fenceline communities living with petrochemical and plastics pollution. The US legislation has gained strong support from the Break Free From Plastic global environmental movement and grass-roots communities of colour, including environmental activists from St James Parish in 'Cancer Alley'.[38] Not surprisingly, it has also faced fierce opposition from the plastics industry. Joshua Baca, vice president of the American Chemistry Council's plastics division, called the bill a 'misguided and harmful piece of legislation'.[39]

It is too early to tell what difference these legislative moves will make. On the one hand, regulators seem to be stuck in a constant game of catch-up, as corporations find ways of anticipating, delaying, and dodging legislation. On the other hand, corporations often see it the other way around, with regulators fast on their heels, threatening their very existence. It is not just the regulators, either: even investors are starting to question the future of plastics in the green transition away from fossil fuels.[40] Could the endgame be on the horizon not only for oil, but also for plastics? It depends on how long corporations can keep pushing the limits of unsustainable growth. There is no question that they will keep on trying. This is where the importance of tackling the 'enablers' comes in.

Challenging the Enablers

In an insightful working paper entitled *Transforming the Global Plastics Economy*, published in 2020, senior policy researchers Diana Barrowclough and Carolyn Deere Birkbeck draw attention to 'the 'missing political economy piece' of evolving global discussions of challenges and responses to plastic pollution. The authors outline the complex field of actors in the global plastics economy, including not only the corporations across the value chain, but also what they call the 'enablers' across the lifecycle of plastics, including 'investors, banks, insurance companies, development banks, and governments that have played a central role in the provision of finance, loans, tax incentives, and insurance'.[41] They point to an important emerging area of policy-relevant research on this topic, which investigates the financial underpinnings of the plastics economy from key enablers. For example, research has shown that extensive state subsidies to the fossil fuel sector have kept the price of virgin plastics feedstocks artificially low and contributed to 'carbon lock-in' across plastics systems, infrastructures, and markets.[42] *The Plastic Waste Makers Index* also uses the language of 'enablers' of the plastics crisis, providing a breakdown of billions of dollars in investments in virgin plastics production from major banks and investors.[43] The less-known role of insurance companies has come to light as well, following the 2019 report *Unwrapping the Risks of Plastic Pollution to the Insurance Industry* by UNEP. The UNEP report is the first study to investigate the role of global insurance companies as underwriters, risk managers, and institutional investors for plastics manufacturers. One of the main findings of the report is that insurers have become increasingly concerned about liability risks related to toxicity, particularly the chemicals involved in plastics that are linked to bodily harms. Phthalates pose 'the single largest potential products liability risk' for insurers because of how widespread these plastics are and how many different kinds of harms they are responsible for.[44] Toxic liability adds to the growing list of ESG investment concerns, dominated by the climate crisis and plastic waste, with echoes of the first toxic scandals that the industry has long fought to bury.

Challenging the enablers of the plastics crisis is more complicated than it might seem. The increasing role of state-owned integrated oil enterprises in Asia and the Middle East, accounting for 30% of the leading plastics producers, illustrates the entanglement of state and industry interests.[45] The geopolitical dimensions of plastics production and consumption are rooted in histories of colonialism, war, and capitalism, with shifting international power relations, particularly the dominance of China. So far, the key policy strategy to address the enablers has been market-driven and focused on financial actors, building on the tools of the climate divestment movement: identifying the financial risks of exposure to liabilities and financial losses, as well as the opportunities for economic growth in more sustainable, circular, and ethical investments.

The increasing awareness among investors and policy-makers that we need to decarbonize virgin plastics production is a promising push factor. However, there is a catch. Most of these proposals take at face value the business-friendly premise of the circular economy for plastics: the idea that it is actually possible to close the loop simply by switching from virgin feedstocks to recycled or bio-based feedstocks. *The Plastic Waste Makers Index*, for example, highlights nine 'concrete examples of genuinely closed-loop recycling projects – where plastic waste is recycled back into new polymers capable of performing the same applications – being built at commercial scale by several of the world's largest polymer producers'.[46] Almost all of these corporate exemplars in the shift towards full 'circularity' are chemical recycling projects. The implication is that the billions of dollars of investments currently being invested in virgin plastics should shift towards these kinds of projects, rewarding the 'leaders' rather than the 'laggards'. However, the report does not mention the considerable greenhouse gas emissions or toxic pollution involved in chemical recycling, nor the technical and cost barriers to developing full-scale chemical recycling systems.[47] It also neglects the question of what it would actually take to decarbonize the plastics industry.

In 2021, research analysts from IRENA published a revealing study showing that decarbonization will be extremely difficult in the petrochemical sector, purely from a technical and economic cost perspective, let alone a political one. In order to achieve decarbonization by 2050, the study found that the petrochemical industry would need to adopt a wide range of technologies and strategies, including renewable energy supply, electrification, CCS, and, to a lesser extent, recycling and energy efficiency measures. In contrast with industry-backed claims that chemical recycling is the only path towards sustainable plastics, the IRENA researchers found that the potentials of chemical recycling and circular economy strategies for decarbonization are highly uncertain, in both technological and financial terms. Furthermore, for recycling to make a difference, it would need to be 'coupled with *deep demand reduction* [emphasis added] and CCS-retrofitted energy recovery'.[48]

Some net zero circular economy proposals for transforming the plastics industry suggest that there should be an overall reduction in plastics production, whether from virgin or recycled feedstocks.[49] However, most policymakers and investors who advocate for decarbonizing plastics agree that the priority is to set clear and measurable targets for reducing virgin plastics production, not overall production, while increasing the recycling, redesign, and reuse of products. In other words, they still have faith in the closed loop of growth through the circular economy.

The Trouble with Growth

There is a fundamental obstacle to limiting plastics production: the dominant paradigm of perpetual economic growth. This has two related implications. First, it means that governments have a strong interest in supporting lucrative markets that boost economic growth, and hence they tend to only restrict markets for compelling reasons, for example in obvious cases where products cause harm to the environment and health. As we have seen, this is what motivates the industry towards wilful ignorance or denial. Throughout the plastics lifecycle, a great number of plastics cause harm to the environment and health, but only a fraction of plastic products have been banned or restricted.[50] Second, it means that economic growth in itself is assumed to be positive, so if certain products are banned due to environmental or health concerns, then the typical solution is to replace them with substitutions. Thus, beverage, food, and other fast-moving consumer goods companies can replace non-recyclable plastic packaging with bioplastics, recycled plastics, recyclable plastics, paper, cardboard, wood, or other substitutions, to comply with most legislation targeting the production of single-use virgin plastic products.

The problem is that the large-scale production of disposable products will put pressure on limited resources, regardless of the material in question. For example, paper is widely seen as a more environmentally sustainable solution than plastic and a viable substitution for many corporations looking to reduce their plastic packaging. However, additional global demand for paper in disposable packaging would put a significant strain on limited forest sources. Forests are already under serious threat from unsustainable logging practices and large-scale tree plantations, which result in natural forest loss and contribute to global heating.[51] Paper recycling faces similar issues to plastic in terms of quality and contamination, and a great deal of paper that should be recycled ends up being incinerated instead. While some corporations have promoted third-party certifications of sustainable forest sources, these certifications do not address the underlying issue of limited forest resources.[52]

There are also issues with substitutions based on bioplastics. First, the term 'bioplastics' is misleading because there is no standard definition: it can be used alternatively to refer to plastic that is bio-based, biodegradable, or compostable.[53] Plastics that are derived from bio-based raw materials, such as sugar, are chemically identical to fossil fuel-based plastics, and thus equally toxic and non-biodegradable. Bioplastics that are marketed as biodegradable or compostable can be derived from either bio-based or fossil fuel-based sources, and they require very high levels of heat in order to break down, which is not available in most municipal compost facilities. Many biodegradable plastics also have chemical additives and thus pose potential health risks. Researchers have pointed to some promising bioplastics applications, but these require further testing as to whether they can be produced safely and sustainably at industrial scales.[54]

There are other trade-offs, too. Synthetic fleece is one of the largest contributors to microplastics in the ocean, with the particles released into water systems in washing machine cycles.[55] However, the fad for merino wool as a natural fabric in outdoor clothing has put tremendous pressure on merino sheep, which are bred to have wrinkly skin in order to yield more wool per animal, and are commonly subjected to a painful form of backside mutilation known as 'mulesing' to prevent attacks from blowflies.[56] Glass also has environmental impacts, due to the use of rare earth minerals and fossil fuels for production, in addition to the carbon emissions from transportation.[57] Furthermore, many glass bottles are not designed for reusability, with higher costs associated with producing reusable seals, and the profits associated with single-use production.[58]

The wool, glass, and pulp and paper industries all have their own trade associations and have lobbied to promote the benefits of their products and to deflect attention from their own unsustainable practices.[59] So, the plastics industry is not unique in this regard, although it has eclipsed the other industries in terms of sheer material abundance, toxicity, and deception. Plastics have succeeded in dominating markets due to their cheapness, versatility, and convenience, while their costs – toxicity, greenhouse gas emissions, and permanent waste – have been deliberately hidden.

What is wrong with encouraging growth in markets for single-use plastic products, as long as they are recycled? Take plastic bottles, for example, which are commonly made out of one of the most recyclable plastics, PET.[60] If we can improve mechanical recycling systems, through separate collection and deposit return schemes, then shouldn't the problem of 'leakage' be resolved for at least these recyclable plastic products? This is the view of many corporations in the beverage and plastics industries, but let's consider the underlying numbers involved. In 2016, the number of plastic bottles produced annually was 480 billion, a figure that is estimated to rise to 583.3 billion in 2021.[61] This is a mind-boggling amount, considering that plastic bottles were only introduced to consumer markets in the 1970s. All the more so given that only a small proportion of these bottles – less than 10% under current systems – have ever been recycled. Even if a greater percentage of bottles could be recycled in the future, most recycled plastics are actually 'downcycled' into less useful or recyclable products, such as plastic bags, because plastic degrades in quality with each round of recycling, leading to industry proposals for chemical recycling 'solutions'. It is not as if there will ever be a perfect circle of half a trillion bottles being converted annually into half a trillion new bottles – and even such an imagined scenario would require considerable greenhouse gas emissions to accomplish such a scale of recycling. Finally, the products that are sold in plastic bottles are, in many cases, harmful rather than beneficial for society – sugary drinks are unhealthy, and so is purified bottled water (due to the lack of minerals).[62] Bottled water, and, worse still, water sold in non-recyclable sachets, has been used as a stop-gap measure in areas without access to clean drinking water, which exacerbates inequalities and sustains inadequate infrastructure.[63]

Since the 1970s oil crisis, the plastics industry has promoted 'lightweighting' as a way of reducing material consumption to save energy use in transportation.[64] According to one plastics representative: 'A consistent theme in resin development over the past 30 years has been new resin grades that allow for thinner walls without sacrificing thermal, mechanical or barrier properties. But gee, doesn't that "compete" with selling more pounds of resin?'[65] The executive is correct in arguing that thinner plastic reduces overall virgin plastics production, but it doesn't prevent billions of plastic bottles from flowing into landfills, incinerators, and the ocean every year. Nor is the incentive for light-weighting entirely environmental: thinner plastic is cheaper to make and transport, and in many cases, it is less recyclable. In January 2020, China introduced a set of new sustainability policies to reduce plastics consumption, including the requirement that thicker plastics be used in many products.[66] Ironically, given the incredible size of the market for plastics in China, this new policy resulted in significant increased demand, at least in the short term, for virgin resins.[67]

The paradigm of perpetual economic growth is incompatible with sustainability, and it is exemplified by the case of single-use plastics. In recent years, a number of scholars and activists have called for 'degrowth' practices of living well with fewer resources and for reviving small-scale local ecologies.[68] Degrowth – a political and ecological philosophy with origins in the 1970s 'limits to growth' debates – criticizes the dominant paradigm of perpetual economic growth on a finite planet.[69] While it has growing appeal, it also remains controversial due to its lack of resonance for communities that face poverty, deindustrialization, and economic marginalization.[70] Many people rely not only on plastic products but also on jobs in the plastics and petrochemical industries, and in the industries that depend on plastics consumption and production. In order to transition away from fossil fuels, many workers, communities, and governments have called for 'just transitions' to protect the livelihoods of displaced fossil fuel workers.[71] Similar dilemmas would be faced in a wider transition away from a plastics-dependent society. While it is crucial to recognize the need for plastics degrowth for the future of life on earth, this also requires acknowledging that there will be many challenges and conflicts on the journey.

Rethinking Systems

In order to tackle the plastics crisis, we need to fundamentally rethink systems of food, retail, construction, transportation, logistics, waste, and countless other industries. This idea is far from new. It has become conventional wisdom that the plastics crisis is a systemic problem requiring systemic change. A number of environmental organizations have pointed to the systemic nature of the plastics crisis, from the 'systemic ignorance' of the climate impacts of plastic pollution,[72] to 'the need to reduce plastic output and push for new systems and models',[73] to the 'myriad ways in which the ongoing climate, public health, air pollution, housing, economic, and systemic racism crises intersect', which have been further exposed by the COVID-19 pandemic.[74]

This raises the question: what kind of systemic change is possible? In principle, many corporations are happy with the idea that the plastics crisis is systemic. If the plastics crisis is a problem with systems rather than particular industries or corporations, then blame can be shifted from one part of the system to another.

Furthermore, corporations across the plastics value chain are well placed to control the development of new systems, given their technical expertise in industrial processes. *The Business Case for a UN Treaty on Plastic Pollution*, endorsed by several leading corporations across the plastics value chain, is premised on the idea that 'coordination is required to drive system change'.[75] The key to the system change that this report is proposing is that it is based on the circular economy illusion that industrial systems can be redesigned to maximize ecological efficiency without fundamentally threatening growth.

The Pew Charitable Trusts and SYSTEMIQ report *Breaking the Plastic Wave* is based on findings from a model of the global plastics system which seek to resolve the challenge that 'a fundamentally systemic problem requires a systemic answer'.[76] The report focuses on six different scenarios up until 2040, ranging from 'Business-as-Usual', with dangerously dystopian plastic waste, to outcomes involving increasing degrees of intervention, to the ultimate 'System Change' scenario, which promises to reduce plastic leakage in the ocean by approximately 80%. The 'System Change' scenario proposes eight systemic interventions: (1) reduce growth in plastics production and consumption through elimination, reuse, and new delivery models (one-third of waste); (2) substitute plastics with paper and compostable materials (one-sixth of waste); (3) design more packaging and other products for recyclability; (4) expand waste collection rates in middle- and low-income countries; (5) double mechanical (versus chemical) recycling capacity globally to 86 million metric tonnes per year; (6) develop 'plastic-to-plastic conversion' (i.e., chemical recycling) to a potential 13 million metric tonnes per year; (7) build facilities to dispose of non-recyclable plastic (23%) as a 'transitional measure'; and (8) reduce plastic waste exports by 90% to low-income countries.[77] These are indeed very dramatic and positive changes to the current system, particularly with the greater focus on reducing production, designing for reuse, and reducing plastic waste exports. In order to create the system change that the report envisions, there would need to be significant changes to legislation and enforcement, on multiple levels, which could only be supported by a global plastics treaty.

Yet the 'System Change' scenario does not challenge unsustainable growth on all fronts, with a strong emphasis on recycling, including chemical recycling, and on substitutions with other materials. To align with the paradigm of economic growth, the report quantifies the economic loss of the 'linear' (traditional, non-circular 'take-waste-make') plastics economy in monetary terms: '95 per cent of aggregate plastic packaging value – US$80 billion–US$120 billion a year – is lost to the economy following a short first-use cycle.'[78] This parallels similar forms of accounting for economic losses in debates about climate policies.[79] The 'System Change' scenario would also fail to decarbonize the plastics economy and would require significant further interventions to reduce greenhouse gas emissions on the scale required to stay within 1.5 degrees of global heating.[80]

The 1972 *Limits to Growth* report to the Club of Rome, and its 1992 successor, were also based on systems modelling, but the authors reached very different conclusions to *Breaking the Plastic Wave*. They did not attempt to soften the blow of the findings by proclaiming that we can have our cake and eat it, too. There are limits to growth on a finite planet, the authors declared, and we are now at the tipping point, beyond the limits of sustainable life on earth.[81]

The plastics crisis is a systemic problem, but this is not to say that individual actions don't make a difference. Quite the contrary. Individuals make up collectives. Limiting individual plastics consumption, switching to reusables, cleaning up litter, calling out corporate irresponsibility, and joining environmental campaigns are all important strategies. Most significantly, individual actions help to counter the cognitive dissonance that comes with living in a plastics-dependent world, to realign ecological values with practical lives under capitalism, and to build communities and social movements that seek alternatives to plastics. On a collective level, the most significant levers for change are to align the plastics crisis more explicitly with the transition away from fossil fuels, and with global environmental justice struggles against environmental racism and waste colonialism.

Halfway Optimism

In the afterword to the paperback edition of *The Uninhabitable Earth*, David Wallace-Wells observes that his book was completed in September 2018 'in a spirit of halfway optimism' about the possibility of a collective human reckoning with the implications of climate science.[82] Paradoxically, the afterword, written after the groundswell of political action over the climate emergency between 2018 and 2019, is far more pessimistic than the rest of the book. One might think that this unprecedented climate activism would have been a cause for further hope, but as Wallace-Wells writes:

> The growing hypocrisy of the truly empowered – corporations, nations, political leaders – illustrates a far more concerning possibility, all the more alarming for being so familiar from other realms of politics: that climate talk could become not a spur to change but an alibi, a cover, for inaction and irresponsibility, the world's

most powerful united in a chorus of double-talk that produces little but song.[83]

As an example of this 'double-talk' around climate change, Wallace-Wells reels off a list of contradictory actions, for example the Canadian Prime Minister Justin Trudeau declaring a climate emergency one day and approving a new oil pipeline the next.

Double-talk is very much alive in the world of plastics, too. The world's biggest plastics producers have signed up to a wide range of voluntary commitments to end plastic waste in the oceans while simultaneously investing billions of dollars in new petrochemical facilities. The largest plastic waste producing countries, such as the United States and the United Kingdom, have signed up to plastic pacts and made commitments to the circular economy while exporting plastic waste to lower-income countries, where it often ends up being illegally burned or dumped.

At least double-talk highlights the contradictions between different courses of action. Another obstacle to tackling the plastics crisis is the constant quest for 'win-win' solutions to reconcile growth with sustainability. Representatives of the Ellen MacArthur Foundation have attempted to reassure petrochemical companies that they can still prosper by joining the New Plastics Economy Global Commitment, 'decoupling' plastics consumption from the use of finite resources so that 'the transition to a circular economy does not impede, but actually contributes to growth'.[84] Plastics producers are not convinced. As noted in chapter 3, only seven plastics producers (i.e., petrochemical companies), representing 4.4% of global plastics production, had signed up to the Global Commitment as of 2020.[85] By contrast, a number of packaging, consumer goods, and beverage firms, including the 'top polluters' Coca-Cola, PepsiCo, Nestlé, and Unilever, have become signatories. However, this isn't necessarily because they are better corporate citizens. Unlike plastics producers, their primary products are not plastics, and as big brands they face high levels of exposure to consumer pressure. Furthermore, the Global Commitment remains voluntary, with no means of holding corporations accountable for meeting their targets, which tend to align with existing corporate sustainability efforts rather than extending beyond them. So far, the main achievement has been to get companies to disclose their total plastic footprint, which tackles important issues of transparency but does not resolve the conflict between growth and sustainability.

Ultimately, there are no sustainable solutions to the plastics crisis that are compatible with perpetual plastics growth. The low-hanging fruit of increasing recycling and banning particular products will scarcely make a dent in the volumes of plastic that are being churned out across the planet. It is wishful thinking to imagine that corporations will voluntarily limit their own unsustainable plastics production. Corporations have demonstrated time and again that they will do whatever it takes to defend and expand their markets.

The more that you look into a crisis that is spiralling out of control, causing the greatest harm and suffering to those who are least responsible, the more difficult it becomes to avoid becoming pessimistic. The surge in disposable plastics during the pandemic has deepened the plastics crisis, and the effects will be felt for many years to come. It may well be irreversible now, combining with climate catastrophe and biodiversity loss as the planet succumbs to the next great mass extinction, whether it occurs within decades or centuries.

Sometimes, though, a crisis can open up real opportunities for collective and systemic change rather than the maintenance of the status quo, revealing the needs and possibilities of such wide-ranging and fundamental transformation. The idea that capitalism will never let a good crisis go to waste assumes that political and economic elites will always gain the upper hand, exploiting opportunities until the end of history.[86] While this idea does have an appeal, I think that it reflects a failure of imagination. There are alternative possibilities for a planetary future that will be free from unlimited plastics growth.

Many books on the plastics crisis offer readers lists of things that they can do about it. I like lists, but I don't have one that I can readily offer. What you can do to rein in the corporations that have fuelled the ecological crisis, simply put, depends on how you are positioned. You can do different kinds of things to address the problem if you are a concerned member of the public, a petrochemical plant worker, a community organizer, a polymer scientist, a lawyer, an institutional investor, a consumer rights advocate, a marine biologist, an international policymaker, or a sociologist. If you are an 'enabler' of harmful plastics production, for example, then you could stop the enabling, although of course it is never as simple as that. Begin by clearly recognizing that you are enabling a destructive system and move on from there to consider the alternatives.

It's easy to say that the plastics crisis is a systemic problem that requires coordinated responses, but in practice this is very difficult to achieve, on multiple levels. Similarly, if you live in a high-income country that consumes and produces high levels of virgin plastics and plastic waste, in a low-income country with plastic pollution problems, or in a fenceline petrochemical community facing toxic exposures, then you will have different capacities and concerns. Form and strengthen alliances and partnerships, across different interest groups and movements, to help build more momentum, connecting your concerns about plastic pollution with the climate crisis, toxic pollution, and systemic racism.

Such multiscalar activism is already underway. Have uncomfortable conversations with people you don't normally talk to, and continually challenge your own as well as others' assumptions and worldviews. Recognize that the plastics crisis is an existential planetary crisis, and act on this knowledge. These are the most important steps we can all take towards achieving a mandate for limiting unsustainable plastics growth.

Notes

Chapter 1 Plastic Unlimited

1 Pew Charitable Trusts and SYSTEMIQ, *Breaking the Plastic Wave: A Comprehensive Assessment of Pathways Towards Stopping Ocean Pollution* (2020).

2 Estimates vary depending on different sources. See: Laura Parker, 'Fast Facts About Plastic Pollution', *National Geographic*, 20 December 2018, at https://www.nationalgeographic.com/science/article/plastics-facts-infographics-ocean-pollution.

3 International Energy Agency, *The Future of Petrochemicals* (2018), at https://www.iea.org/reports/the-future-of-petrochemicals.

4 Andrew Inkpen and Kannan Ramaswamy, 'Breaking Up Global Value Chains: Evidence from the Oil and Gas Industry', *Advances in International Management*, 30 (2017): 55–80.

5 Mark Eramo, 'Global Chemical Industry Outlook: Assessing Today's Strong Markets and Preparing for the 2020s', IHS Markit, 3 August 2018, at https://ihsmarkit.com/research-analysis/global-chemical-industry-outlook-2020.html.

6 Divy Malik, Parth Manchanda, Theo Jan Simons, and Jeremy Wallach, 'The Impact of COVID-19 on the Global Petrochemical Industry', McKinsey, 28 October 2020, at https://www.mckinsey.com/industries/chemicals/our-insights/the-impact-of-covid-19-on-the-global-petrochemical-industry.

7   Zhou Peng, Theo Jan Simons, Jeremy Wallach, and Adam Youngman, 'Petrochemicals 2020: A Year of Resilience and the Road to Recovery', McKinsey, 21 May 2021, at https://www.mckinsey.com/industries/chemicals/our-insights/petrochemicals-2020-a-year-of-resilience-and-the-road-to-recovery.

8   Author's field notes, virtual World Petrochemical Conference, 8–12 March 2021.

9   Parker, 'Fast Facts About Plastic Pollution'.

10 Plastic Soup Foundation, Facts & Figures, at https://www.plasticsoupfoundation.org/en/plastic-facts-and-figures; Sarah Zhang, 'Half of All Plastic Was Made in the Past 13 Years', *The Atlantic*, 19 July 2017, at https://www.theatlantic.com/science/archive/2017/07/plastic-age/533955.

11 See Ian Tiseo, 'Cumulative Plastic Production Volume Worldwide from 1950 to 2050', Statista, 27 January 2021, at https://www.statista.com/statistics/1019758/plastics-production-volume-worldwide; Ellen MacArthur Foundation, with the support of the World Economic Forum, *The New Plastics Economy: Rethinking the Future of Plastics & Catalysing Action* (2017), at https://www.ellenmacarthurfoundation.org/publications/the-new-plastics-economy-rethinking-the-future-of-plastics-catalysing-action.

12 Lisa A. Hamilton, Steven Feit, Carroll Muffett, et al., *Plastic and Climate: The Hidden Costs of a Plastic Planet* (Center for International Environmental Law, 2019). Other estimates put this figure at 98%: see Dominic Charles, Laurent Kimman, and Nakul Saran, *The Plastic Waste Makers Index* (Minderoo Foundation, 2021), at https://www.minderoo.org/plastic-waste-makers-index/findings/executive-summary/.

13 Other petrochemical products include pesticides, adhesives, synthetic textiles, rubbers, dyes, fertilizers, and synthetic paints and coatings. Eren Cetinkaya, Nathan Liu, Theo Jan Simons, and Jeremy Wallach, 'Petrochemicals 2030: Reinventing the Way to Win in a Changing Industry', *Chemicals: Our Insights*, 21 February 2018, at https://www.mckinsey.com/industries/

chemicals/our-insights/petrochemicals-2030-reinventing-the-way-to-win-in-a-changing-industry.

14 Charles et al., *The Plastic Waste Makers Index*.

15 David Azoulay, Priscilla Villa, Yvette Arellano, et al., *Plastic and Health: The Hidden Cost of a Plastic Planet* (Center for International Environmental Law, 2019).

16 Pierpaolo Mudu, Benedetto Terracini, and Marco Martuzzi, *Human Health in Areas with Industrial Contamination* (WHO Regional Office for Europe, 2014).

17 See Sara M. Wiebe, *Everyday Exposure: Indigenous Mobilization and Environmental Justice in Canada's Chemical Valley* (UBC Press, 2016); Beverly Wright, 'Race, Politics and Pollution: Environmental Justice in the Mississippi River Chemical Corridor', in *Just Sustainabilities: Development in an Unequal World*, eds Julian Agyeman, Robert D. Bullard, and Bob Evans (MIT Press, 2003), pp. 125–45.

18 Elisabeth Mendenhall, 'Oceans of Plastic: A Research Agenda to Propel Policy Development', *Marine Policy*, 96 (2018): 291–8.

19 Karen McVeigh, 'Coca-Cola, Pepsi and Nestlé Named Top Plastic Polluters for Third Year in a Row', *Guardian*, 7 December 2020, at https://www.theguardian.com/environment/2020/dec/07/coca-cola-pepsi-and-nestle-named-top-plastic-polluters-for-third-year-in-a-row.

20 Charles et al., *The Plastic Waste Makers Index*.

21 Anja Krieger, 'Nobody Knows How Much Plastic and Fish Will Swim in the Ocean by 2050', 20 March 2019, at https://www.riffreporter.de/de/umwelt/fakten check-plastik-fisch; Leo Hornak, 'Will There Be More Fish or Plastic in the Sea in 2050?' *BBC News Magazine*, 15 February 2016, at https://www.bbc.co.uk/news/magazine-35562253.

22 See chapter 2.

23 See chapter 4.

24 Prachi Patel, 'Stemming the Plastic Tide: 10 Rivers Contribute Most of the Plastic in the Oceans', *Scientific American*, 1 February 2018, at https://www.scientificamerican.com/article/stemming-the-plastic-tide-

10-rivers-contribute-most-of-the-plastic-in-the-oceans. The ten rivers finding was overturned by another study in 2021, which showed that 1,000 small and medium-sized rivers, rather than large rivers, accounted for 80% of the plastic waste flowing into oceans, all from five countries in Asia, but the basic point about geography remained. See Lourens J. J. Meijer, Tim van Emmerik, Ruud van der Ent, Christian Schmidt, and Laurent Lebreton, 'More than 1000 Rivers Account for 80% of Global Riverine Plastic Emissions into the Ocean', *Science Advances*, 7(18), 30 April 2021, at https://advances.sciencemag.org/content/7/18/eaaz5803.

25　Alliance to End Plastic Waste, 'Launching the Alliance to End Plastic Waste', London, 16 January 2019, at https://www.youtube.com/watch?v=MOfF6SUT0nY.

26　Kate O'Neill, 'Can the World Win the War on Plastic?' *World Politics Review*, 10 March 2020, at https://www.worldpoliticsreview.com/articles/28590/having-polluted-the-oceans-plastics-are-now-facing-a-popular-backlash.

27　Aarushi Jain, 'Trash Trade Wars: Southeast Asia's Problem with the World's Waste', *Council on Foreign Relations 100*, 8 May 2020, at https://www.cfr.org/in-brief/trash-trade-wars-southeast-asias-problem-worlds-waste; Yen Nee Lee, 'Malaysia, Following in China's Footsteps, Bans Plastic Waste Imports', CNBC, 25 January 2019, at https://www.cnbc.com/2019/01/25/climate-change-malaysia-following-china-bans-plastic-waste-imports.html.

28　The concept of 'waste colonialism' will be discussed in further detail in the next chapter. See also David Naguib Pellow, *Resisting Global Toxics: Transnational Movements for Environmental Justice* (MIT Press, 2007); Max Liboiron, 'Waste Colonialism', *Discard Studies*, 1 November 2018, at https://discardstudies.com/2018/11/01/waste-colonialism/.

29　Lucy Siegle, *Turning the Tide on Plastic: How Humanity (And You) Can Make Our Globe Clean Again* (Orion Publishing, 2018); Will McCallum, *How to Give Up Plastic: A Guide to Changing the World, One Plastic Bottle at a Time* (Penguin, 2018); Martin Dorey, *No.*

More. Plastic.: What You Can Do to Make a Difference – the #2minutesolution (Penguin, 2018); The F Team, *F**k Plastic: 101 Ways to Free Yourself from Plastic and Save the World* (Seven Dials, 2018).

30 Alice Delemare Tangpuori, George Harding-Rolls, Nusa Urbancic, and Ximena Purita Banegas Zallio, *Talking Trash: The Corporate Playbook of False Solutions to the Plastics Crisis* (Changing Markets Foundation, 2021); Greenpeace, *Throwing Away the Future: How Companies Still Have It Wrong on Plastic Pollution 'Solutions'*, 30 September 2019, at https://www.greenpeace.org/usa/research/how-companies-still-have-it-wrong-on-plastic-pollution-solutions; Break Free From Plastic, 'Missing the Mark: Unveiling Corporate False Solutions to the Plastic Pollution Crisis', 21 June 2021, at https://www.breakfreefromplastic.org/missing-the-mark-unveiling-corporate-false-solutions-to-the-plastic-crisis/.

31 Author's field notes, petrochemical markets workshop, London, 25–7 September 2018.

32 Jeffrey Meikle, *American Plastic* (Rutgers University Press, 1995), p. 3.

33 Lloyd Stouffer, 'Plastics Packaging: Today and Tomorrow', Report presented to the National Plastics Conference, The Society of the Plastics Industry, 1963.

34 Roland Barthes, *Mythologies*, trans. Annette Lavers (Hill and Wang, 1972), p. 111.

35 The plastics executive is quoted in Susan Freinkel, *Plastic: A Toxic Love Story* (Dreamscape Media, 2011), p. 6.

36 Plastics Europe, *Plastics – the Facts 2020: An Analysis of European Plastics Production, Demand and Waste Data*, accessed online on 27 April 2021 but no longer available.

37 See Freinkel, *Plastic*; Siegle, *Turning the Tide on Plastic*.

38 Rebecca Altman, 'The Myth of Historical Bio-based Plastics', *Science*, 373 (2021): 47–9 (p. 48).

39 Altman, 'The Myth of Historical Bio-based Plastics'; see also John Tully, *The Devil's Milk: A Social History of Rubber* (NYU Press, 2011).

40   Paul David Blanc, *Fake Silk: The Lethal History of Viscose Rayon* (Yale University Press, 2016), p. ix.

41   Author's field notes, petrochemical markets workshop, London, 25–7 September 2018.

42   Alfred D. Chandler, *Shaping the Industrial Century: The Remarkable Story of the Modern Chemical and Pharmaceutical Industries* (Harvard University Press, 2005); Michael Reubold, Sean Milmo, and Martin Todd, *Petrochemicals and EPCA: A Passionate Journey* (European Petrochemical Association, 2016).

43   For the role of the Second World War in shaping the petrochemical and plastics industry, see Chandler, *Shaping the Industrial Century*; Freinkel, *Plastic*; and Gerald E. Markowitz and David Rosner, *Deceit and Denial: The Deadly Politics of Industrial Pollution* (University of California Press, 2002).

44   Rebecca Altman, 'Time-Bombing the Future', *Aeon*, 2 January 2019, at https://aeon.co/essays/how-20th-century-synthetics-altered-the-very-fabric-of-us-all; see also Freinkel, *Plastic*, p. 25.

45   Markowitz and Rosner, *Deceit and Denial*, p. 140.

46   Florian Jessberger, 'On the Origins of Individual Criminal Responsibility under International Law for Business Activity: IG Farben on Trial', *Journal of International Criminal Justice*, 8 (2010): 783–802. See also Werner Abelshauser, Wolfgang von Hippel, Jeffrey Allan Johnson, and Raymond G. Stokes, *German Industry and Global Enterprise: BASF: The History of a Company* (Cambridge University Press, 2003); Diarmuid Jeffreys, *Hell's Cartel: IG Farben and the Making of Hitler's War Machine* (Macmillan, 2008).

47   Jeffreys, *Hell's Cartel*, p. 232.

48   Jessberger, 'On the Origins of Individual Criminal Responsibility'.

49   Hubert Buch-Hansen and Lasse Folke Henriksen, 'Toxic Ties: Corporate Networks of Market Control in the European Chemical Industry, 1960–2000', *Social Networks*, 58 (2019): 24–36; see also Chandler, *Shaping the Industrial Century*.

50   Plastics Europe Deutschland e.V. and Fachgruppe

Makromolekulare Chemie in der Gesellschaft Deutscher Chemiker e.V. (GDCh), '100 Years of Plastic: Unlimited Possibilities for the Future', at http://www.100yearsofplastics.com.

51 Plastics Europe Deutschland e.V. and Fachgruppe Makromolekulare Chemie in der Gesellschaft Deutscher Chemiker e.V. (GDCh), 'Plastics During the Pandemic', at https://www.100jahrekunststoffe.de/en/2020/12/plastics-during-the-pandemic.

52 Samantha Maldonado and Marie J. French, 'Plastics Industry Goes After Bag Bans During Pandemic', *Politico*, 24 April 2020, at https://www.politico.com/states/new-jersey/story/2020/03/24/plastics-industry-goes-after-bag-bans-during-pandemic-1268843. See the discussion in chapter 5.

53 Michelle Meagher, *Competition Is Killing Us: How Big Business Is Harming Our Society and Planet – and What to Do About It* (Penguin 2020), p. 111.

54 Meagher, *Competition Is Killing Us*, p. 95.

55 Business Roundtable, 'Business Roundtable Redefines the Purpose of a Corporation to Promote "an Economy That Serves All Americans"', 19 August 2019, at https://www.businessroundtable.org/business-roundtable-redefines-the-purpose-of-a-corporation-to-promote-an-economy-that-serves-all-americans.

56 Joel Bakan, *The New Corporation: How 'Good' Corporations Are Bad for Democracy* (Vintage Books, 2020), pp. 29, 33. Reflecting on how the corporation has changed since he wrote the bestselling book *The Corporation* in 2003, Bakan argues that 'despite all the posturing, the corporation's character remains fundamentally the same. ... It's still a psychopath – just a more charming one now' (pp. 57–8).

57 Peter Dauvergne, *Will Big Business Destroy Our Planet?* (Polity, 2018). Several other social scientists have written about the business of corporate environmental responsibility and private-led sustainability initiatives. For example, see Stefano Ponte, *Business, Power and Sustainability in a World of Global Value Chains* (Zed Books, 2019); David L. Levy and Peter Newell, *The*

Business of Global Environmental Governance (MIT Press, 2005).

58   Tangpuori et al., *Talking Trash*; Greenpeace, *Throwing Away the Future*.

59   Tangpuori et al., *Talking Trash*.

60   Diana Barrowclough and Carolyn Deere Birkbeck, *Transforming the Global Plastics Economy: The Political Economy and Governance of Plastics Production and Pollution* (GEG Working Paper No. 142, 2020), at https://www.econstor.eu/handle/10419/224117; Charles et al., *The Plastic Waste Makers Index*.

61   Chandler, *Shaping the Industrial Century*.

62   Plastics Europe, *Plastics – the Facts 2020*; Plastics Industry Association, *Size and Impact Report 2020*, at https://www.plasticsindustry.org/sizeandimpact.

63   Chandler, *Shaping the Industrial Century*.

64   Chemical and Engineering News, Global Top 50 for 2020, https://cen.acs.org/business/finance/CENs-Global-Top-50-2020/98/i29.

65   Charles et al., *Plastic Waste Makers Index*, p. 13.

66   GlobalData, 'China to Contribute 28% of Global Petrochemical Capacity Additions by 2030', 30 October 2020, at https://www.globaldata.com/china-contribute-28-global-petrochemical-capacity-additions-2030-says-globaldata.

67   International Energy Agency, *The Future of Petrochemicals*.

68   Sandra Eckert, 'Varieties of Framing the Circular Economy and the Bioeconomy: Unpacking Business Interests in European Policymaking', *Journal of Environmental Policy & Planning*, 23(2) (2021): 181–93.

69   Barrowclough and Deere Birkbeck. *Transforming the Global Plastics Economy*, p. 31.

70   See chapter 3.

71   Linsey McGoey, *The Unknowers: How Strategic Ignorance Rules the World* (Zed Books, 2019); Hannah Jones, *Violent Ignorance: Confronting Racism and Migration Control* (Zed Books, 2020).

72   Robert D. Bullard, *Dumping in Dixie: Race, Class, and Environmental Quality* (Routledge, 2018); Brendan

Coolsaet, ed., *Environmental Justice: Key Issues* (Routledge, 2020).
73 Bakan, *The New Corporation*, p. 34.
74 Mariana Mazzucato, *The Value of Everything: Making and Taking in the Global Economy* (Hachette UK, 2018), p. 271.
75 See Alex Serpo, 'Don't Let this Recycling Crisis Go to Waste', *Waste Review*, 3 April 2018, at https://wastemanagementreview.com.au/five-programs-nwric/; Guillaume Gruère, 'Never Let a Good Water Crisis Go to Waste', OECD, 21 March 2019, at https://www.oecd.org/agriculture/never-waste-a-good-water-crisis.
76 Rahm Emanuel, 'Opinion: Let's Make Sure This Crisis Doesn't Go to Waste', *Washington Post*, 25 March 2020, at https://www.washingtonpost.com/opinions/2020/03/25/lets-make-sure-this-crisis-doesnt-go-waste.
77 Bernard Looney, Keynote Address, IP Week, 22 February 2020, at https://www.bp.com/content/dam/bp/business-sites/en/global/corporate/pdfs/news-and-insights/speeches/bernard-looney-keynote-address-ip-week.pdf.
78 Philip Mirowski, *Never Let a Serious Crisis Go to Waste: How Neoliberalism Survived the Financial Meltdown* (Verso, 2013).
79 Naomi Klein, *The Shock Doctrine: The Rise of Disaster Capitalism* (Macmillan, 2007).
80 Joseph Masco, 'The Crisis in Crisis', *Current Anthropology*, 58(S15) (2017): S65–76 (p. S65).
81 Max Liboiron, *Pollution Is Colonialism* (Duke University Press, 2021), p. 12.
82 Matt Hern and Am Johal, *Global Warming and the Sweetness of Life: A Tar Sands Tale* (MIT Press, 2019), p. 23.
83 Oliver Smith and Avi Brisman. 'Plastic Waste and the Environmental Crisis Industry', *Critical Criminology*, 29 (2021): 289–309 (p. 289).
84 Damian Carrington, 'Why the Guardian Is Changing the Language It Uses About the Environment', *Guardian*, 17 May 2019, at https://www.theguardian.com/environment/2019/may/17/why-the-guardian-is-changing-the-language-it-uses-about-the-environment.

85 Michelle Langrand, 'A New Global Treaty to Tackle Plastic Pollution?' Geneva Solutions, 1 March 2021, at https://genevasolutions.news/sustainable-business-finance/a-new-global-treaty-to-tackle-plastic-pollution.
86 Publicly available materials include corporate documents, speeches, magazines, blogs, websites, interviews, videos, media and NGO reports, and secondary sources. The observations at industry events and related interviews with corporate representatives were conducted between 2016 and 2021 as part of two research projects on environmental justice and the petrochemical industry, funded by the European Research Council (grant no. 639583) and the Leverhulme Trust (Philip Leverhulme Prize). All interviews were conducted with prior and informed consent, and names of interviewees have been anonymized. Observations from events anonymize corporate statements, unless (as many are) these are also publicly available in corporate conference reports, in magazines, and on websites.

Chapter 2 Manufacturing Toxic Wants and Needs

1 For example, see Freinkel, *Plastic*; Siegle, *Turning the Tide on Plastic*.
2 Christine Hoeg Hanson, 'The Debate About Plastics Should Be More Realistic', Danish Plastics Federation, 2 October 2020, at https://plast.dk/en/2020/10/the-debate-about-plastics-should-be-more-realistic.
3 Plastics Industry Association, 'So, You Want to Stop Making Plastics. What Happens Afterward?' 1 April 2020, at https://www.plasticsindustry.org/blog/so-you-want-stop-making-plastics-what-happens-afterward.
4 This widely held view of early plastics has been questioned by some scholars, who argue that the extent to which plastics alleviated actual material shortages is unclear. See Liboiron, *Pollution Is Colonialism*, p. 2.
5 For an incisive account of the Big Tobacco playbook, see Naomi Oreskes and Erik M. Conway, *Merchants of Doubt: How a Handful of Scientists Obscured the Truth on Issues from Tobacco Smoke to Global Warming* (Bloomsbury, 2011).

6   Markowitz and Rosner, *Deceit and Denial*.
7   Wiebe, *Everyday Exposure*; Michelle Murphy, 'Chemical Infrastructures of the St Clair River', in *Toxicants, Health and Regulation since 1945*, eds Soraya Boudia and Nathalie Jas (Routledge, 2013), pp. 103–15.
8   See Wright, 'Race, Politics and Pollution'; Barbara Allen, *Uneasy Alchemy: Citizens and Experts in Louisiana's Chemical Corridor Disputes* (MIT Press, 2003); Merrill Singer, 'Down Cancer Alley: The Lived Experience of Health and Environmental Suffering in Louisiana's Chemical Corridor', *Medical Anthropology Quarterly*, 25(2) (2011): 141–63; Thom Davies, 'Slow Violence and Toxic Geographies: "Out of Sight" to Whom?' *Environment and Planning C* (2019), at https://doi.org/10.1177/2399654419841063.
9   Azoulay et al., *Plastic and Health*; Alice Mah, *Petrochemical Planet: Multiscalar Battles of Industrial Transformation* (Duke University Press, forthcoming).
10 Reubold et al., *Petrochemicals and EPCA*, p. 29.
11 For a classic text describing the early growth of the petrochemical industry, see Barry Commoner, *The Closing Circle: Nature, Man, and Technology* (Bantam Books, 1971).
12 See Alice Mah, 'Toxic Legacies and Environmental Justice', in *Environmental Justice: Key Issues*, ed. Brendan Coolsaet (Routledge, 2020), pp. 121–31.
13 Adam Hanieh, 'Petrochemical Empire: The Geo-politics of Fossil-Fuelled Production', *New Left Review* 130 (2021): 25–51 (p. 44).
14 See chapters 4 and 6 for discussions of 'limits to growth' and 'degrowth' debates.
15 Barry Commoner, 'The Once and Future Threat of the Petrochemical Industry to the World of Life,' *New Solutions*, 11 (1) (2001): 1–12 (p. 6).
16 Quoted in Freinkel, *Plastic*, p. 142.
17 See Susan Strausser, *Waste and Want: A Social History of Trash* (Holt, 2000); Meikle, *American Plastic*.
18 Freinkel, *Plastic*, p. 142.
19 Author's field notes, European Petrochemical Conference, Rotterdam, 6–7 February 2018.

20   A fascinating book on the rise of the plastic water bottle is Gay Hawkins, Emily Potter, and Kane Race, *Plastic Water: The Social and Material Life of Bottled Water* (MIT Press, 2015).

21   Meikle, *American Plastic*.

22   Author's field notes, petrochemical markets workshop, Rotterdam, 7 February 2018.

23   David Michaels, *Doubt Is Their Product: How Industry's Assault on Science Threatens Your Health* (Oxford University Press, 2008), p. 61.

24   Freinkel, *Plastic*, pp. 81–114.

25   Author's field notes, petrochemical markets workshop, London, 25–7 September 2018.

26   For accessible reviews of the scientific and health debates on DEHP in blood bags, see Jody A. Roberts, 'Reflections of an Unrepentant Plastiphobe: An Essay on Plasticity and the STS Life', in *Accumulation: The Material Politics of Plasticity*, eds Gay Hawkins, Jennifer Gabrys, and Mike Michael (Routledge, 2013), pp. 121–33; and Freinkel, *Plastic*, chapter 4.

27   See Freinkel, *Plastic*, pp. 107–8.

28   Markowitz and Rosner, *Deceit and Denial*, chapters 6 and 7.

29   Regarding the vinyl chloride scandal, Michaels observed that 'the manipulation of science by the plastics industry was at least as self-serving and flagrant as the behavior of any other industry I have cited'. Michaels, *Doubt Is Their Product*, p. 34.

30   Plastics Association, 'PLASTICS Response to the American Academy of Pediatrics (AAP) Policy Statement Regarding the Use of Plastic Food Packaging', 24 July 2018, at https://www.plasticsindustry.org/article/plastics-response-american-academy-pediatrics-aap-policy-statement-regarding-use-plastic.

31   Michaels, *Doubt Is Their Product*, p. 65.

32   Author's field notes, petrochemical markets workshop, Rotterdam, 7 February 2018.

33   Phil Brown, Vanessa De La Rosa, and Alissa Cordner, 'Toxic Trespass: Science, Activism, and Policy Concerning Chemicals in Our Bodies', in *Toxic Truths: Environmental*

Justice and Citizen Science in a Post-Truth Age, eds Thom Davies and Alice Mah (Manchester University Press, 2020), pp. 34–58.

34 DuPont Lawsuits (re PFOA pollution in USA); Business and Human Rights Resource Centre, at https://www.business-humanrights.org/en/latest-news/dupont-lawsuits-re-pfoa-pollution-in-usa.

35 'PDOA Added to Stockholm Convention', 27 May 2019, at https://www.chemanager-online.com/en/news/pfoa-added-stockholm-convention-pop-list; UN Stockholm Convention, 'Overview', at http://www.pops.int/TheConvention/Overview/tabid/3351/Default.aspx.

36 Brown et al., 'Toxic Trespass', p. 47.

37 Brown et al., 'Toxic Trespass', p. 47.

38 Laura Sullivan, 'Transcript: Plastic Wars', Frontline and NPR, 31 March 2020, at https://www.pbs.org/wgbh/frontline/film/plastic-wars/transcript/.

39 Sullivan, 'Transcript: Plastic Wars'.

40 Tony Radoszewski, Plastics Industry Association Response to Frontline and NPR: Plastic Wars, 1 April 2020, at https://www.plasticsindustry.org/article/plastics-industry-association-response-frontline-npr-plastic-wars.

41 Matthew Naitove, 'Why "Plastic Wars" Got Me Riled', *Plastics Technology*, 6 April 2020, at https://www.ptonline.com/blog/post/why-plastic-wars-got-me-riled.

42 Bakan, *The New Corporation*, p. 33.

43 Freinkel, *Plastic*, p. 162.

44 Samantha MacBride, *Recycling Reconsidered: The Present Failure and Future Promise of Environmental Action in the United States* (MIT Press, 2011), p. 220.

45 Emily C. Dooley and Carl MacGowan, 'Long Island's Infamous Garbage Barge of 1987 Still Influences Laws', *NewsDay*, 17 March 2017, at https://projects.newsday.com/long-island/long-island-garbage-barge-left-islip-30-years-ago.

46 For example, Kate O'Neill, *Waste* (Polity, 2019); Liboiron, *Pollution Is Colonialism*; Hamilton et al., *Plastic and Climate*.

47 Sara Ann Wylie, *Fractivism: Corporate Bodies and Chemical Bonds* (Duke University Press, 2018); Diane

M. Sicotte, 'From Cheap Ethane to a Plastic Planet: Regulating an Industrial Global Production Network', *Energy Research & Social Science*, 66 (2020): 101479; Azoulay et al., *Plastic and Health*.

48 Hamilton et al., *Plastic and Climate*.

49 Peter Dauvergne, *Environmentalism of the Rich* (MIT Press, 2016), pp. 46–7.

50 See Catherine Liamson, Sherma Benosa, Miko Aliño, and Beau Baconguis, *Sachet Economy: Big Problems in Small Packets* (Global Alliance for Incinerator Alternatives, 2020).

51 Plastics Europe, *Plastics – the Facts 2020*.

52 Alice Mah and Xinhong Wang, 'Accumulated Injustices of Environmental Justice: Living and Working with Petrochemical Pollution in Nanjing, China', *Annals of the American Association of Geographers* 109(6) (2019): 1961–77.

53 Max Liboiron, 'There's No Such Thing as "We"', *Discard Studies*, 12 October 2020, at https://discard studies.com/2020/10/12/theres-no-such-thing-as-we.

54 Research assistant's field notes, Louisiana, 24 April 2018.

55 Author's interview with petrochemical engineer, Antwerp, 17 January 2019.

56 Author's interview with petrochemical industry representative, Brussels, 31 May 2016.

57 Author's field notes, plastics industry webinar, November 2020.

58 Rebecca Altman, 'On Wishcycling', *Discard Studies*, 15 February 2021, at https://discardstudies.com/2021/02/15/on-wishcycling.

Chapter 3 The Corporate Alliance to (Never) End Plastic Waste

1 Ellen MacArthur Foundation, *The New Plastics Economy*; Pew Charitable Trusts and SYSTEMIQ, *Breaking the Plastic Wave*.

2 Author's field notes, Future of Polyolefins Conference, Antwerp, 16 January 2019.

3 Plastics Europe, *Plastics 2030: Plastics Europe's Voluntary Commitment to Increasing Circularity and*

Resource Efficiency, accessed online on 15 October 2020 but no longer available.

4   Fiona Harvey, 'Industry Alliance Sets Out $1bn to Tackle Oceans' Plastic Waste', *Guardian*, 16 January 2019, at https://www.theguardian.com/environment/2019/jan/16/ industry-alliance-sets-out-1bn-to-tackle-oceans-plastic-waste.

5   International Energy Agency, *The Future of Petro-chemicals*.

6   Hamilton et al., *Plastic and Climate*.

7   Dewey Johnson and R.J. Chang, 'Crude Oil-to-Chemicals Projects Presage a New Era in Global Petrochemical Industry', IHS Markit, 6 August 2018, at https:// ihsmarkit.com/research-analysis/crudeoil-chemicals-projects.html.

8   Mark Thomas, 'Crude Oil-to-Chemicals: A Game Changer for the Chemical Industry', *Chemical Week*, 29 November 2019, at https://chemweek.com/CW/ Document/107708/Crude-oiltochemicals-A-game-changer-for-the-chemical-industry.

9   Laxmi Haigh, 'A Who's Who of Companies Investing in Plastic Production: Is the Alliance to End Plastic Waste Hypocritical?' *Packaging Insights*, 13 January 2019, at https://www.packaginginsights.com/news/a-whos-who-of-companies-investing-in-plastic-production-is-the-alliance-to-end-plastic-waste-hypocritical.html.

10 Alliance to End Plastic Waste, at https://endplasticwaste. org.

11 O'Neill, *Waste*, pp. 156–9.

12 Pellow, *Resisting Global Toxics*; Liboiron, 'Waste Colonialism'.

13 Karl W. Kenyon and Eugene Kridler, 'Laysan Albatrosses Swallow Indigestible Matter', *Auk*, 86(2) (1969): 339–43; Peter Ryan, 'A Brief History of Marine Litter Research', in *Marine Anthropogenic Litter*, eds Melanie Bergmann, Lars Gutow, and Michael Klages (Springer Nature, 2015), pp. 1–28.

14 Study Panel on Assessing Potential Ocean Pollutants, *Assessing Potential Ocean Pollutants* (National Academy of Sciences, 1975).

15   Steven Feit, *Fuelling Plastics: Plastic Industry Awareness of the Ocean Plastics Problem* (Centre for International Environmental Law, 2017).

16   Jennifer Clapp, 'The Rising Tide Against Plastic Waste: Unpacking Industry Attempts to Influence the Debate', in *Histories of the Dustheap: Waste, Material Cultures, Social Justice*, eds Stephanie Foote and Elizabeth Mazzolini (MIT Press, 2012), pp. 199–225.

17   Jennifer Clapp and Linda Swanston, 'Doing Away with Plastic Shopping Bags: International Patterns of Norm Emergence and Policy Implementation', *Environmental Politics*, 18(3) (2007): 315–32; Peter Dauvergne, 'Why Is the Global Governance of Plastic Failing the Oceans?' *Global Environmental Change*, 51 (2018): 22–31.

18   Clapp, 'The Rising Tide Against Plastic Waste', p. 200.

19   Christine Figgener, 'What I Learnt Pulling a Straw Out of a Turtle's Nose', *Nature*, 563, no. 7730 (2018): 157–8.

20   Author's interview with a petrochemical representative, Antwerp, 16 January 2019.

21   Ellen MacArthur Foundation. 'What Is a Circular Economy?' at https://ellenmacarthurfoundation.org/topics/circular-economy-introduction/overview.

22   Ellen MacArthur Foundation, *The New Plastics Economy*.

23   European Commission, *European Strategy for Plastics in a Circular Economy* (2018).

24   Corporate Europe Observatory, 'Plastic Promises: Industry Seeking to Avoid Binding Regulations', 22 May 2020, at https://corporateeurope.org/en/power-lobbies/2018/05/plastic-promises.

25   Author's field notes, Future of Polyolefins Conference, Antwerp, 16 January 2019.

26   Michael Pooler, 'INEOS Announces Antwerp for €3bn Investment', *Financial Times*, 15 January 2019, at https://www.ft.com/content/8df66d84-18d6-11e9-9e64-d150b3105d21.

27   Some definitions of the circular economy place reduction at the top of the 'waste hierarchy' among the different 'Rs', and recycling at the bottom. See Julian Kirchherr, Denise Reike, and Marko Hekkert, 'Conceptualizing

the Circular Economy: An Analysis of 114 Definitions', *Resources, Conservation and Recycling*, 127 (2017): 221–32.

28 O'Neill, *Waste*, chapter 6.

29 Sandra Eckert, *Corporate Power and Regulation: Consumers and the Environment* (Palgrave Macmillan, 2019), p. 104.

30 Corporate Europe Observatory, 'Plastic Promises'.

31 European Commission, *European Strategy for Plastics*. The Ellen Macarthur Foundation has since stressed in the Global Commitment the importance of moving beyond recycling, including Extended Producer Responsibility, a subject that will be addressed in chapter 6.

32 Author's field notes, virtual World Petrochemical Conference, 8–12 March 2021.

33 These seven producers were BASF SE, Borealis AG, Eastman, Indorama Ventures Public Company Limited, Kingfa Sci. & Tech. Co., NOVAPET, and Plasticos Compuestos S.A., the Ellen MacArthur Foundation, *Global Commitment 2020 Progress Report*, with input from the UN Environment Programme, at https://www.newplasticseconomy.org/assets/doc/Global-Commitment-2020-Progress-Report.pdf.

34 Author's interview with a catalyst engineer, petrochemical company, Antwerp, 17 January 2019.

35 Tim Sykes, 'Chemical Recycling 101', *Packaging Europe*, 28 February 2018, at https://packagingeurope.com/chemical-recycling-101-plastic-waste.

36 European Commission, 'Closing the Loop: Commission Delivers on Circular Economy Action Plan', press release, 4 March 2019, at https://ec.europa.eu/commission/presscorner/detail/en/IP_19_1480.

37 Maurizio Crippa, Bruno De Wilde, Rudy Koopmans, et al., *A Circular Economy for Plastics: Insights from Research and Innovation to Inform Policy and Funding Decisions*, ed. Michiel De Smet and Mats Linder (European Commission, 2019), p. 10.

38 Crippa et al., *A Circular Economy for Plastics*, p. 140.

39 Sykes, 'Chemical Recycling 101'.

40 Crippa et al., *A Circular Economy for Plastics*, p. 140.

41 Kaushik Mitra and Mark Morgan, 'Is Chemical Recycling a Game Changer?' IHS Markit, 9 August 2019, at https://ihsmarkit.com/research-analysis/is-chemical-recycling-a-game-changer.html.

42 Kim Ragaert, Laurens Delva, and Kevin Van Geem, 'Mechanical and Chemical Recycling of Solid Plastic Waste', *Waste Management*, 69 (2017): 24–58; Clayton Huggett and Barbara C. Levin, 'Toxicity of the Pyrolysis and Combustion Products of Poly(Vinyl Chlorides): A Literature Assessment', *Fire and Materials*, 11(3) (1987): 131–42.

43 Azoulay et al., *Plastic and Health*.

44 Wiebe, *Everyday Exposure*; Wright, 'Race, Politics, and Pollution'.

45 David N. Pellow, *Resisting Global Toxics: Transnational Movements for Environmental Justice* (MIT Press, 2007), p. 9.

46 Lawrence Summers, quoted in Pellow, *Resisting Global Toxics*, p. 9.

47 Pellow, *Resisting Global Toxics*, p. 10.

48 Mitra and Morgan, 'Is Chemical Recycling a Game Changer?'

49 Rageart et al., 'Mechanical and Chemical Recycling'; Huggett and Levin, 'Toxicity of the Pyrolysis of Solid Waste'.

50 O'Neill, *Waste*, p. 11.

51 Together, China and Hong Kong imported 72.4% of all plastic waste, with Hong Kong acting as the entry port into China. Amy L. Brooks, Shunli Wang, and Jenna R. Jambeck, 'The Chinese Import Ban and Its Impact on Global Plastic Waste Trade', *Science Advances* 4(6) (2018): eaat0131.

52 Joshua Goldstein, *Remains of the Everyday: A Century of Recycling in Beijing* (University of California Press, 2020).

53 Global Alliance for Incinerator Alternatives, *Discarded: Communities on the Frontlines of the Global Plastic Crisis* (2019), p. 10; Cody Boteler, 'ISRI: No "Panacea" on Import Restrictions – What China Wants Is More Complicated', *Waste Dive*, 2 April 2018, at https://

www.wastedive.com/news/china-situation-scrap-import-green-fence-national-sword-blue-sky/520306.

54 O'Neill, 'Can the World Win the War on Plastic?'
55 Laura Parker, 'China's Ban on Trash Imports Shifts Waste Crisis to Southeast Asia', *National Geographic*, 16 November 2018, at https://www.nationalgeographic.com/environment/article/china-ban-plastic-trash-imports-shifts-waste-crisis-southeast-asia-malaysia; Cheryl Katz, 'Piling Up: How China's Ban on Importing Waste Has Stalled Global Recycling', *Yale Environment 360*, 7 March 2019, at https://e360.yale.edu/features/piling-up-how-chinas-ban-on-importing-waste-has-stalled-global-recycling.
56 See Pellow, *Resisting Global Toxics*; Liboiron, 'Waste Colonialism'.
57 Pellow, *Resisting Global Toxics*, p. 9.
58 O'Neill, 'Can the World Win the War on Plastic?'
59 Stuart J. Barnes, 'Out of Sight, Out of Mind: Plastic Waste Exports, Psychological Distance and Consumer Plastic Purchasing', *Global Environmental Change*, 58 (2019): 101943.
60 See Katharina Kummer, *International Management of Hazardous Wastes: The Basel Convention and Related Legal Rules* (Oxford University Press, 1999).
61 Goldstein, *Remains of the Everyday*.
62 'Adam Minter: In the Flow of Things', *Discard Studies*, 5 June 2019, at https://discardstudies.com/2019/05/06/adam-minter-how-things-flow. See also Adam Minter, *Junkyard Planet: Travels in the Billion-Dollar Trash Trade* (Bloomsbury, 2013).
63 'Adam Minter: In the Flow of Things'.
64 Liboiron capitalizes 'Land' as a way of 'referring to the unique entity that is the combined living spirit of plants, animals, air, water, humans, histories, and events recognized by many Indigenous communities', as contrasted with colonial views of land as common and universal (*Pollution Is Colonialism*, p. 7). I follow this usage only when referring to the particular idea of Land as a sink, to highlight the implications of waste colonialism.
65 Liboiron, 'Waste Colonialism'.

66 Haigh, 'A Who's Who of Companies Investing in Plastic Production'.

67 Perry Wheeler, 'Industry Group Seeks to Maintain Single-Use Plastic Status Quo', Greenpeace, 14 January 2019, at https://www.greenpeace.org/usa/news/industry-group-seeks-to-maintain-single-use-plastic-status-quo.

68 Charles McDermid, 'Dozens of Companies Launch US$1 Billion Bid to End Plastic Pollution in Asia but Environmentalists Dismiss it as "Greenwashing" Stunt', Break Free From Plastic, 2 February 2019, at https://www.breakfreefromplastic.org/2019/02/13/companies-bid-end-plastic-pollution-asia-greenwashing-stunt.

69 Alliance to End Plastic Waste, 'Launching the Alliance to End Plastic Waste', London, 16 January 2019, at https://www.youtube.com/watch?v=MOfF6SUT0nY.

70 The basis for this 'fact' will be critically discussed in chapter 4.

71 Safripol, 'Conversation with the Alliance to End Plastic Waste', Dialogue on Sustainability, 6 March 2020, at https://www.youtube.com/watch?v=QgYrJB_dlbs.

72 World Plastics Council, 'WPC Recommendation on the "Proposals to Amend Parts of the Basel Convention, Considered at the 14th Conference of the Parties"', at https://www.worldplasticscouncil.org/issue-positions/basel-convention.

73 Bob Patel, quoted in Alliance to End Plastic Waste, 'Launching the Alliance to End Plastic Waste'.

74 Safripol, 'Conversation with the Alliance to End Plastic Waste'.

75 Safripol, 'Conversation with the Alliance to End Plastic Waste'.

76 Alliance to End Plastic Waste, 'Closing the Loop in Accra, Ghana', 19 February 2021, at https://www.youtube.com/watch?v=7Jcptc7k5ds.

77 Cole Rosengren, 'Unilever Tests New Recycling Method for Plastic Pouches in Indonesia', *Waste Dive*, 15 May 2017, at https://www.wastedive.com/news/unilever-tests-new-recycling-method-for-plastic-pouches-in-indonesia/442716/.

78 Alliance to End Plastic Waste, *Progress Report 2020*

(Alliance to End Plastic Waste, 2020), at https:// endplasticwaste.org/progress-report/.

79 See, for example, O'Neill, *Waste*; Hong Yang, Mingguo Ma, Julian R. Thompson, and Roger J. Flower, 'Waste Management, Informal Recycling, Environmental Pollution and Public Health', *Journal of Epidemiology and Community Health*, 72(3) (2018): 237–43.

80 Goldstein, *Remains of the Everyday*; Minter, *Junkyard Planet*.

81 Louis Gore-Langton, 'Greenpeace Chief: Alliance to End Plastic Waste Is Misfiring, as Exposé Reveals Flagship Project Failure,' *Packaging Insights*, 22 January 2021, at https://www.packaginginsights.com/news/ alliance-to-end-plastic-waste-fires-back-at-greenpeace-over-criticism-of-flagship-project-failure.html.

Chapter 4 Hedging Against Climate Risk

1 David Wallace-Wells, *The Uninhabitable Earth: A Story of the Future* (Penguin, 2019), p. 151.

2 Richard Stafford and Peter J.S. Jones, 'Viewpoint – Ocean Plastic Pollution: A Convenient but Distracting Truth?' *Marine Policy*, 103 (2019): 187–91.

3 Corey J. A. Bradshaw, Paul R. Ehrlich, Andrew Beattie, et al. 'Underestimating the Challenges of Avoiding a Ghastly Future', *Frontiers in Conservation Science*, 13 January 2021, at https://doi.org/10.3389/fcosc.2020.615419.

4 Author's interview with petrochemical industry representative, Brussels, 3 May 2016.

5 International Energy Agency, *The Future of Petrochemicals*; author's field notes, European Petrochemical Conference, Rotterdam, 6–7 February 2018.

6 Valérie Masson-Delmotte, Panmao Zhai, Hans-Otto Pörtner, et al., *Global Warming of 1.5°C: An IPCC Special Report* (IPCC, 2018).

7 Hamilton et al., *Plastic and Climate*.

8 See Oreskes and Conway, *Merchants of Doubt*.

9 Clapp and Swanston, 'Doing Away with Plastic Shopping Bags'.

10 Nicholas Kusnetz, 'What Does Net Zero Emissions Mean

for Big Oil? Not What You'd Think', *Inside Climate News*, 16 July 2020, at https://insideclimatenews.org/news/16072020/oil-gas-climate-pledges-bp-shell-exxon/.

11 International Energy Agency, *Oil 2021* (2021), at https://www.iea.org/reports/oil-2021.

12 Quote from webinar discussion, 'The Future's Not in Plastics', Climate Week New York City, 24 September 2020, at https://carbontracker.org/climate-week-nyc-2020-webinar-the-futures-not-in-plastic-benjamin/.

13 Hamilton et al., *Plastic and Climate*. The report excluded emissions sources from other petrochemical products, including fillers, plasticizers, and additives, while noting that these are often used in the manufacture of single-use plastics.

14 Hamilton et al., *Plastic and Climate*, p. 11.

15 Pew Charitable Trusts and SYSTEMIQ, *Breaking the Plastic Wave*, p. 44.

16 International Renewable Energy Agency, *Reaching Net Zero* (2020), p. 73.

17 Carbon emissions from petrochemical products (primarily plastics) come not only from direct energy and emissions processes during production, roughly 1.7 Gt per year in 2018, but also from product use phase emissions (0.2 Gt/yr); emissions from decomposition or incineration processes (around 0.24 Gt/yr); and a further 1 Gt per year which is stored in hydrocarbon products and could be released in the future. See International Renewable Energy Agency, *Reaching Net Zero*, p. 72.

18 Bradshaw et al., 'Underestimating the Challenges', p. 4.

19 Bradshaw et al., 'Underestimating the Challenges', p. 6.

20 Donella H. Meadows, Dennis L. Meadows, Jørgen Randers, and William W. Behrens III, *The Limits to Growth: A Report to the Club of Rome* (Universe Books, 1972).

21 Donella H. Meadows, Dennis L. Meadows, and Jørgen Randers, *Beyond the Limits: Global Collapse or a Sustainable Future* (Earthscan Publications Ltd, 1992); Donella Meadows, Jørgen Randers, and Dennis Meadows, *Limits to Growth: The 30-Year Update* (Chelsea Green Publishing, 2004).

22 See Neela Banerjee, John H. Cushman Jr, David Hasemyer, and Lisa Song, *Exxon: The Road Not Taken* (Inside Climate News, 2015), at https://insideclimatenews.org/book/exxon-the-road-not-taken; Oreskes and Conway, *Merchants of Doubt*.

23 Banerjee et al., *Exxon: The Road Not Taken*.

24 Banerjee et al., *Exxon: The Road Not Taken*.

25 Marco Grasso, 'Oily Politics: A Critical Assessment of the Oil and Gas Industry's Contribution to Climate Change', *Energy Research & Social Science*, 50 (2019): 106–115.

26 International Energy Agency, *The Oil and Gas Industry in Energy Transitions* (IEA, 2020), at https://www.iea.org/reports/the-oil-and-gas-industry-in-energy-transitions.

27 IP Week, London, 2021, at https://www.ipweek.co.uk/.

28 Charles et al., *The Plastic Waste Makers Index*; Barrowclough and Deere Birkbeck, *Transforming the Global Plastics Economy*.

29 Hamilton et al., *Plastic and Climate*; Charles et al., *The Plastic Waste Makers Index*.

30 Pablo Giorgi, 'Reinventing the Refinery Through the Energy Transition and Refining-Petrochemical Integration', IHS Markit, 11 February 2021, at https://ihsmarkit.com/research-analysis/energy-transition-and-petchem-integration.html.

31 International Energy Agency, *Oil 2021*, p. 4.

32 International Energy Agency, *The Future of Petrochemicals*, p. 11

33 International Energy Agency, *The Future of Petrochemicals*, p. 3.

34 David Roberts, 'The International Energy Agency Continually Underestimates Wind and Solar Power. Why?' *Vox*, 12 October 2015, at https://www.vox.com/2015/10/12/9510879/iea-underestimate-renewables.

35 Robert W. Howarth, 'Methane Emissions and Climatic Warming Risk from Hydraulic Fracturing and Shale Gas Development: Implications for Policy', *Energy and Emission Control Technologies*, 3 (2015): 45–54.

36 Irja Vormedal, Lars H. Gulbrandsen, and Jon Birger Skjærseth, 'Big Oil and Climate Regulation: Business as

Usual or a Changing Business?' *Global Environmental Politics*, 20(4) (2020): 143–66.

37   Rick Lord et al., *Plastics and Sustainability: A Valuation of Environmental Benefits, Costs and Opportunities for Continuous Improvement*, funded by the American Chemistry Council (Trucost, 2016).

38   Safripol, 'Conversation with the Alliance to End Plastic Waste'.

39   Clapp and Swanston, 'Doing Away with Plastic Shopping Bags'.

40   McKinsey, *Innovations for Greenhouse Gas Reductions*, commissioned by the International Council of Chemical Associations (McKinsey, 2009), accessed online on 22 March 2021 but no longer available.

41   Author's field notes, IP Week, London, February 2020.

42   Looney, Keynote Address, IP Week, 22 February 2020.

43   Nicholas Kusnetz, 'Two US Oil Companies Join Their European Counterparts in Making Net-Zero Pledges', *Inside Climate News*, 12 November 2020, at https://insideclimatenews.org/news/12112020/two-us-oil-companies-join-their-european-counterparts-making-net-zero-pledges.

44   ExxonMobil, Energy and Carbon Summary, at https://corporate.exxonmobil.com/Sustainability/Emissions-and-climate#.

45   Mike Coffin, 'Net-Zero Goals for Oil Companies Do Not Tell the Whole Story', *Financial Times*, 25 June 2020, at https://www .ft.com/content/07497357-5c39-4dea-839f-b33691dc7195; David Tong, *Big Oil Reality Check* (Oil Change International, 2020); Kusnetz, 'What Does Net Zero Emissions Mean for Big Oil?'

46   However, as we will see, corporate-led 'science-based targets' and 'global sustainability standards' for net zero were later developed, echoing corporate responses to the circular economy for plastics.

47   United Nations, Race to Zero Campaign, at https://unfccc.int/climate-action/race-to-zero-campaign.

48   Masson-Delmotte et al., *Global Warming of 1.5°C: An IPCC Special Report*.

49   World Business Council for Sustainable Development,

'WBCSD Raises the Bar for Sustainable Business Leadership', 26 October 2020, at https://www.wbcsd.org/Overview/News-Insights/General/News/WBCSD-raises-the-bar-for-sustainable-business-leadership.

50 Author's field notes, virtual World Petrochemical Conference, 8–12 March 2021.

51 David Carlin, 'Climate Leaders Are Aligning to Net Zero: What Does This Commitment Mean?' *Forbes*, 28 April 2021, at https://www.forbes.com/sites/davidcarlin/2021/04/28/climate-leaders-are-aligning-to-net-zero-what-does-this-commitment-mean; United Nations Climate Change, 'Commitments to Net Zero Double in Less Than a Year', Press Release, 21 September 2021, at https://unfccc.int/news/commitments-to-net-zero-double-in-less-than-a-year; Tong, *Big Oil Reality Check*; Oliver Milman, 'Biden Vows to Slash Emissions by Half to Meet "Existential Crisis of Our Times"', *Guardian*, 22 April 2021, at https://www.theguardian.com/us-news/2021/apr/22/us-emissions-climate-crisis-2030-biden.

52 Author's field notes as COP26 observer, Glasgow, 1–12 November 2021.

53 Owen Walker and Camilla Hodgson, 'Carney-Led Finance Coalition Has up to $130tn Funding Committed to Hitting Net Zero', *Financial Times*, 3 November 2021, at https://www.ft.com/content/8f7323c8-3197-4a69-9fcd-1965f3df40a7.

54 'Net Zero Smoke and Mirrors, a Story of Betrayal: Making the Case Against Carbon Market Offsetting', 8 November 2021, at https://www.youtube.com/watch?v=QywPKXwesi0&ab_channel=UnitedNationsClimateChangeCOP26.

55 Matt McGrath, 'COP26: Fossil Fuel Industry Has Largest Delegation at Climate Summit', BBC News, 8 November 2021, available at https://www.bbc.co.uk/news/science-environment-59199484.

56 Matthew Taylor, 'No Formal Cop26 Role for Big Oil Amid Doubts Over Firms' Net Zero Plans', *Guardian*, 21 October 2021, available at https://www.theguardian.com/environment/2021/oct/21/

no-formal-cop26-role-for-big-oil-amid-doubts-over-firms-net-zero-plans

57 Damian Gammell, CEO, 'Reaching Net Zero Greenhouse Gas Emissions by 2040', Coca-Cola, 7 December 2020, at https://www.cocacolaep.com/media/news/2020/net-zero-ceo-comment-damian-gammell.

58 Katherine Dunn, 'Procter & Gamble Says It Will Go Climate Neutral by 2050', *Fortune*, 16 July 2020, at https://fortune.com/2020/07/16/emissions-climate-neutral-procter-and-gambler.

59 Jim Cornall, 'Top of Form Bottom of Form Amcor to Help Brands Communicate Packaging Carbon Footprint Reductions', *Daily Reporter*, 14 January 2021, at https://www.dairyreporter.com/Article/2021/01/14/Amcor-to-help-brands-communicate-packaging-carbon-footprint-reductions.

60 Novolex, Sustainability Report 2020, available at https://novolex.com/wp-content/uploads/2020-Novolex-Sustainability-Report.pdf.

61 Berry Global, 'Berry Global Announces Science-Based Targets to Cut Operational and Supply Chain Emissions', 20 April 2021, at https://ir.berryglobal.com/news-releases/news-release-details/berry-global-announces-science-based-targets-cut-operational-and.

62 Ellen MacArthur Foundation, *Completing the Picture: How the Circular Economy Tackles Climate Change* (Ellen MacArthur Foundation, 2019), at https://www.ellenmacarthurfoundation.org/publications/completing-the-picture-climate-change.

63 Naoko Ishii, 'The Next Decade Is Critical for the Climate. Here's How the Circular Economy Can Help', World Economic Forum, 1 March 2021, at: https://www.weforum.org/agenda/2021/03/how-the-circular-economy-can-help-the-climate.

64 Eramo, 'Global Chemical Industry Outlook'.

Chapter 5 Plastics in the Pandemic

1 Author's interview with polymer scientist, Coventry, UK, 10 May 2019.

2 Sidney Gross, quoted in Meikle, *American Plastic*, p. 272.
3 Sidney Gross, quoted in Meikle, *American Plastic*, p. 271.
4 Costanza Musu, 'War Metaphors Used for COVID-19 Are Compelling But Also Dangerous', *The Conversation*, 8 April 2020, at https://theconversation.com/war-metaphors-used-for-covid-19-are-compelling-but-also-dangerous-135406.
5 Fredric Bauer and Germain Fontenit, 'Plastic Dinosaurs – Digging Deep into the Accelerating Carbon Lock-in of Plastics', *Energy Policy*, 156 (2021): 112418; Deger Saygin and Dolf Gielen, 'Zero-Emission Pathway for the Global Chemical and Petrochemical Sector', *Energies* 14(13) (2021): 3772; Charles et al., *The Plastic Waste Makers Index*.
6 Samantha Maldonado and Marie J. French, 'Plastics Industry Goes After Bag Bans During Pandemic', *Politico*, 24 April 2020, at https://www.politico.com/states/new-jersey/story/2020/03/24/plastics-industry-goes-after-bag-bans-during-pandemic-1268843; Tridibesh Dey and Mike Michael, 'Driving Home "Single-Use": Plastic Politics in the Times of the COVID-19', *Discover Society*, 30 April 2020, at https://discoversociety.org/2020/04/30/driving-home-single-use-plastic-politics-in-the-times-of-the-covid-19; Nils Johannsen, 'Disaster Capitalism, COVID-19, and Single-Use Plastic', *Antipode Online*, 26 January 2021, at https://antipode-online.org/2021/01/26/covid-19-and-single-use-plastic.
7 Peng et al., 'Petrochemicals 2020'; author's field notes, virtual World Petrochemical Conference, 8–12 March 2021.
8 Author's field notes, virtual World Petrochemical Conference, 8–12 March 2021.
9 Author's field notes, Future of Polyolefins Conference, Antwerp, 16 January 2019.
10 Author's field notes, virtual World Petrochemical Conference, 7–14 April 2020.
11 Author's field notes, virtual World Petrochemical Conference, 7–14 April 2020.
12 Author's field notes, virtual World Petrochemical Conference, 8–12 March 2021.
13 Peng et al., 'Petrochemicals 2020'; author's field notes,

virtual World Petrochemical Conference, 8–12 March 2021.

14 Peng et al., 'Petrochemicals 2020'; author's field notes, virtual World Petrochemical Conference, 8–12 March 2021.

15 Peng et al., 'Petrochemicals 2020'.

16 Author's field notes, virtual World Petrochemical Conference, March 8-12, 2021.

17 Dey and Michael, 'Driving Home "Single-Use"'; Johannsen, 'Disaster Capitalism, COVID-19, and Single-Use Plastic'.

18 Maldonado and French, 'Plastics Industry Goes After Bag Bans During Pandemic'.

19 Ian Schlegel and Connor Gibson, 'The Making of an Echo Chamber: How the Plastic Industry Exploited Anxiety About COVID-19 to Attack Reusable Bags' (Greenpeace, 2020), at https://www.greenpeace.org/usa/research/how-the-plastic-industry-exploited-anxiety-about-covid-19.

20 Neeltje van Doremalen, Trenton Bushmaker, Dylan H. Morris, et al., 'Aerosol and Surface Stability of SARS-CoV-2 as Compared with SARS-CoV-1', *New England Journal of Medicine* 382(16) (2020): 1564–7.

21 Packaging Europe, 'EuPC Calls for Postponement of Single-Use Plastic Directive', 14 April 2020, at https://packagingeurope.com/eupc-calls-for-postponement-of-single-use-plastic-directive.

22 Estelle Eonnet, '#BreakFreeFromPlastic Sent an Open Letter to the European Commission – Here's What It Says', Break Free From Plastic, 24 April 2020, at https://www.breakfreefromplastic.org/2020/04/24/breakfreefromplastic-open-letter-european-commission.

23 João Pinto da Costa, 'The 2019 Global Pandemic and Plastic Pollution Prevention Measures: Playing Catch-Up', *Science of the Total Environment*, 774 (2021): 145806.

24 Perry Wheeler, 'Over 115 Health Experts Sign Statement Addressing Safety of Reusables During COVID-19', Greenpeace, 22 June 2020, at https://www.greenpeace.org/usa/news/over-115-health-experts-sign-statement-addressing-safety-of-reusables-during-covid-19.

25 Da Costa, 'The 2019 Global Pandemic and Plastic Pollution Prevention'.

26 Jacob Duer, 'The Plastic Pandemic Is Only Getting Worse During COVID-19', World Economic Forum, 1 July 2020, at https://www.weforum.org/agenda/2020/07/plastic-waste-management-covid19-ppe; Adam Vaughn, 'The Plastic Pandemic', *New Scientist*, 247(3295) (2020) at https://doi.org/10.1016/S0262-4079(20)31391-9; Joe Brock, 'Plastic Pandemic: Covid-19 Trashed the Recycling Dream', Reuters, 5 October 2020, at https://www.reuters.com/investigates/special-report/health-coronavirus-plastic-recycling.

27 Hiroko Tabuchi, Michael Corkery, and Carlos Mureithi, 'Big Oil Is in Trouble: Its Plan: Flood Africa with Plastic Waste', *New York Times*, 30 August 2020, at https://www.nytimes.com/2020/08/30/climate/oil-kenya-africa-plastics-trade.html; American Chemistry Council, 'Chemicals and Plastics Industry Corrects Record on Its Position Regarding US–Kenya Trade Negotiations', Press Release, 31 August 2020, at https://www.americanchemistry.com/Media/Press ReleasesTranscripts/ACC-news-releases/Chemicals-and-Plastics-Industry-Corrects-Record-on-Its-Position-Regarding-US-Kenya-Trade-Negotiations.html.

28 Beth Gardiner, 'In Pandemic Recovery Efforts, Polluting Industries Are Winning Big', *Yale Environment 360*, 23 June 2020, at https://e360.yale.edu/features/in-pandemic-recovery-efforts-polluting-industries-are-winning-big; Fiona Harvey, 'US Fossil Fuel Giants Set for a Coronavirus Bailout Bonanza', *Guardian*, 12 May 2020, at https://www.theguardian.com/environment/2020/may/12/us-fossil-fuel-companies-coronavirus-bailout-oil-coal-fracking-giants-bond-scheme.

29 Author's field notes, virtual World Petrochemical Conference, 8–12 March 2021.

30 Author's field notes, virtual World Petrochemical Conference, 8–12 March 2021.

31 Clapp, 'The Rising Tide Against Plastic Waste'; Liboiron, *Pollution Is Colonialism*.

32 Olivier Coutard and Elizabeth Shove, 'Infrastructures,

Practices, and the Dynamics of Demand', in *Infrastructures in Practice: The Dynamics of Demand in Networked Societies*, eds Elizabeth Shove and Frank Trentmann (Routledge, 2018), pp. 10–22 (p. 14).

33 Kara Lavender Law, Natalie Starr, Theodore R. Siegler, Jenna R. Jambeck, Nicholas J. Mallos, and George H. Leonard, 'The United States' Contribution of Plastic Waste to Land and Ocean', *Science Advances* 6(44) (2020): eabd0288; see also Damian Carrington, 'US and UK Citizens are World's Biggest Sources of Plastic Waste – Study', *Guardian*, 30 October 2020, at https://www.theguardian.com/environment/2020/oct/30/us-and-uk-citizens-are-worlds-biggest-sources-of-plastic-waste-study; Charles et al., *The Plastic Waste Makers Index*.

34 Plastics Insight, 'Global Consumption of Plastic Materials by Region (1980–2015)', Market Statistics, 14 March 2016, at https://www.plasticsinsight.com/global-consumption-plastic-materials-region-1980-2015.

35 Neha Parashar and Subrata Hait, 'Plastics in the Time of COVID-19 Pandemic: Protector or Polluter?' *Science of the Total Environment*, 759 (2021): 144274; Md Sazzadul Haque, Shariar Uddin, Sayed Md Sayem, and Kazi Mushfique Mohib, 'Coronavirus Disease 2019 (COVID-19) Induced Waste Scenario: A Short Overview', *Journal of Environmental Chemical Engineering*, 9(1) (2020): 104660.

36 Parashar and Hait, 'Plastics in the Time of COVID-19 Pandemic', p. 4.

37 Haque et al., 'Coronavirus Disease 2019 (COVID-19) Induced Waste Scenario'.

38 'Covid-19 Has Posed New Challenges to the World's Waste-Pickers', *The Economist*, 19 December 2020, at https://www.economist.com/international/2020/12/19/covid-19-has-posed-new-challenges-to-the-worlds-waste-pickers; 'Philippine Trash Trawlers Struggle with Virus-Led Plastic Surge', *Al Jazeera*, 10 August 2020, at https://www.aljazeera.com/economy/2020/8/10/philippine-trash-trawlers-struggle-with-virus-led-plastic-surge.

39 Examples include: Nicola DeBlasio and Phoebe Fallon, *Avoiding a Plastic Pandemic: The Future of Sustainability in a Post COVID-19 World* (Belfer Center for Science and International Affairs, Harvard Kennedy School, 2021); Tridibesh Dey, 'COVID-19 as Method: Managing the Ubiquity of Waste and Waste-Collectors in India', *Journal of Legal Anthropology*, 4(1) (2020): 76–91; Marc Kalina and Elizabeth Tilley, '"This Is Our Next Problem": Cleaning Up from the COVID-19 Response', *Waste Management*, 108 (2020): 202–5; Jie Han and Shanshan He, 'Urban Flooding Events Pose Risks of Virus Spread During the Novel Coronavirus (COVID-19) Pandemic', *Science of the Total Environment*, 755 (2021): 142491.
40 Greenpeace, *Trashed: How the UK Is Still Dumping Plastic Trash on the Rest of the World* (2021), at https://www.greenpeace.org.uk/resources/trashed-plastic-report.
41 Marc Kalina, Fathima Ali, and Elizabeth Tilley, '"Everything Continued as Normal": What Happened to Africa's Wave of Covid-19 Waste?' *Waste Management*, 120 (2021): 277–9.
42 See, for example, Elizabeth Claire Alberts, 'Sharks Are Polluted with Plastic, New Study Shows', *EcoWatch*, 12 August 2020, at https://www.ecowatch.com/shark-plastic-stomach-2646956951.html; Jim Robbins, 'Why Bioplastics Will Not Solve the World's Plastic Problem', *Yale Environment 360*, 31 August 2020, at https://e360.yale.edu/features/why-bioplastics-will-not-solve-the-worlds-plastics-problem; Joe Brock, 'The Plastic Pandemic: COVID-19 Trashed the Recycling Dream', Reuters, 5 October 2020, at https://www.reuters.com/investigates/special-report/health-coronavirus-plastic-recycling/; Layal Liverpool, 'Plastic Baby Bottles Shed Millions of Plastics When Shaken', *New Scientist*, 19 October 2020, at https://www.newscientist.com/article/2257599-plastic-baby-bottles-shed-millions-of-microplastics-when-shaken/; Justine Calma, 'Amazon Generates Millions of Pounds of Plastic Waste', *The Verge*, 15 December 2020, at https://www.theverge.com/2020/12/15/22174990/

amazon-packaging-millions-pounds-plastic-waste-oceans-pollution-oceana; Damian Carrington, 'Airborne Plastic Pollution "Spiralling Around the Globe", Study Finds', *Guardian*, 12 April 2021, at https://www.theguardian.com/environment/2021/apr/12/airborne-plastic-pollution-spiralling-around-the-globe-study-finds; Olivia Rosane, 'Ocean Plastic Pollution Flows Through More Rivers than Previously Thought', *EcoWatch*, 3 May 2021, at https://www.ecowatch.com/ocean-plastic-pollution-rivers-source-2652861436.html; Emma Love, 'Plastic Pollution to Cost Society $7.1 Trillion by 2040', *Resource*, 8 September 2021, at https://resource.co/article/plastic-pollution-cost-society-71-trillion-2040#:~:text=A%20new%20report%20by%20WWF,urgent%20action%20is%20not%20taken.&text=As%20plastic%20is%20a%20very,a%20significant%20period%20of%20time.; Melina Spanoudi, 'Is a UN Treaty Needed to Stop Plastic Pollution?', *Packaging Europe*, 9 September 2021, at https://packagingeurope.com/new-white-paper-published-by-ellen-macarthur-foundation/.

43 Timothy Morton, *Being Ecological* (Pelican Books, 2018), p. 8.

44 Tangpuori et al., *Talking Trash*, pp. 74–5.

45 McVeigh, 'Coca-Cola, Pepsi and Nestlé Named Top Plastic Polluters'.

46 Rich Gower, Joanne Green, and Mari Williams, *The Burning Question: Will Companies Reduce Their Plastic Use?* (Tearfund, 2020), at https://learn.tearfund.org/-/media/learn/resources/reports/2020-tearfund-the-burning-question-en.pdf.

47 Charles et al., *The Plastic Waste Makers Index*.

48 Schlegel and Gibson, 'The Making of an Echo Chamber'.

49 Oceana, *Amazon's Plastic Problem Revealed* (Oceana, 2021), at https://plastics.oceana.org/campaign/amazon; see also Calma, 'Amazon Generates Millions of Pounds of Plastic Waste'.

50 Research assistant's field notes, World Petrochemical Conference, San Antonio, Texas, 19 March 2019.

51 Pew Charitable Trusts and SYSTEMIQ, *Breaking the Plastic Wave*, p. 8.
52 Carbon Tracker, *The Future's Not in Plastics: Why Plastics Demand Won't Rescue the Oil Sector*, 4 September 2020, at https://carbontracker.org/reports/the-futures-not-in-plastics/.
53 Charles et al., *The Plastic Waste Makers Index*.
54 Nils Simon, Karen Raubenheimer, Niko Urho, et al., 'A Binding Global Agreement to Address the Life Cycle of Plastic', *Science*, 373(6550) (2021): 43–7.
55 See the discussion on plastics and waste colonialism in chapter 3.
56 Author's field notes, virtual World Petrochemical Conference, 8–12 March 2021.

Chapter 6 How Can We Curb the Plastics Crisis?

1 Aaron Raubvogel, *Tackling the Plastic Crisis with the Break Free From Plastic Pollution Act*, Centre for International Environmental Law, 11 February 2020, at https://www.ciel.org/tackling-the-plastic-crisis-with-the-break-free-from-plastic-pollution-act; Liboiron, *Pollution Is Colonialism*.
2 Dave Ford, 'We Need a Paris Agreement for Plastics', *Scientific American*, 30 December 2020, at https://www.scientificamerican.com/article/we-need-a-paris-agreement-for-plastics.
3 Peter Dauvergne, 'Why Is the Global Governance of Plastic Failing the Oceans?' *Global Environmental Change*, 51 (2018): 22–31.
4 João Pinto da Costa, Catherine Mouneyrac, Mónica Costa, Armando C. Duarte, and Teresa Rocha-Santos, 'The Role of Legislation, Regulatory Initiatives and Guidelines on the Control of Plastic Pollution', *Frontiers in Environmental Science*, 24 July 2020, at https://doi.org/10.3389/fenvs.2020.00104.
5 Michelle Langrand, 'A New Global Treaty to Tackle Plastic Pollution?' Geneva Solutions, 1 March 2021, at https://genevasolutions.news/sustainable-business-finance/a-new-global-treaty-to-tackle-plastic-pollution.

6   Ford, 'We Need a Paris Agreement for Plastics'.
7   World Wildlife Fund (WWF), the Ellen MacArthur Foundation, and Boston Consulting Group (BCG), *The Business Case for a UN Treaty on Plastic Pollution*, 2020, at https://www.plasticpollutiontreaty.org/UN_treaty_plastic_poll_report.pdf.
8   Langrand, 'A New Global Treaty to Tackle Plastic Pollution?'
9   Simon et al., 'A Binding Global Agreement to Address the Life Cycle of Plastic'.
10 Raubvogel, *Tackling the Plastic Crisis*.
11 David Azoulay, quoted in Langrand, 'A New Global Treaty to Tackle Plastic Pollution?'
12 Tallash Kantai, *Confronting the Plastic Pollution Pandemic*, Still One Earth Briefing No. 8 (International Institute for Sustainable Development, 2020).
13 Susan Shaw, quoted in David A. Taylor, 'We're Facing an Uncertain Plastic Future', *Discover Magazine*, 1 May 2021, at https://www.discovermagazine.com/environment/were-facing-an-uncertain-plastic-future.
14 Theo Colborn, 'The Fossil Fuel Connection', *EarthFocus*, 1 October 2013, Link TV, at https://www.youtube.com/watch?v=5hhHefhmozU.
15 Raubvogel, *Tackling the Plastic Crisis*.
16 Katy Harsant, *Selective Responsibility: History, Power and Politics in the United Nations*, PhD dissertation, University of Warwick, 2016.
17 United Nations, 'Environmental Racism in Louisiana's "Cancer Alley", Must End, Say UN Human Rights Experts', *UN News*, 2 March 2021, at https://news.un.org/en/story/2021/03/1086172.
18 Juliano Calil, Marce Gutiérrez-Graudiņš, Steffanie Munguía, and Christopher Chin, *Neglected: Environmental Justice Impacts of Marine Litter and Plastic Pollution* (UNEP, 2021).
19 Rob Nixon, *Slow Violence and the Environmentalism of the Poor* (Harvard University Press, 2011), p. 2.
20 Davies, 'Slow Violence and Toxic Geographies', p. 6.
21 Liboiron, 'Waste Colonialism'.
22 Global Alliance for Incinerator Alternatives, *Discarded*, p. 10; Boteler, 'ISRI: No "Panacea" on Import Restrictions'.

23 See O'Neill, 'Can the World Win the War on Plastic?'
24 Bakan, *The New Corporation*.
25 Jane Thier, 'Moving from Value to Values: An ESG Assessment', *WasteDive*, 28 May 2021, at https://www.wastedive.com/news/moving-from-value-to-values-esg-assessment/600990.
26 Mazzucato, *The Value of Everything*.
27 OECD, 'Extended Producer Responsibility', at https://www.oecd.org/env/tools-evaluation/extendedproducer-responsibility.htm.
28 See Carl Dalhammar, 'Industry Attitudes Towards Ecodesign Standards for Improved Resource Efficiency', *Journal of Cleaner Production*, 123 (2016): 155–66; Nathan Kunz, Kieren Mayers, and Luk N. Van Wassenhove, 'Stakeholder Views on Extended Producer Responsibility and the Circular Economy', *California Management Review*, 60(3) (2018): 45–70.
29 Kunz and Wassenhove, 'Stakeholder Views on Extended Producer Responsibility'.
30 Avalon Diggle and Tony R. Walker, 'Implementation of Harmonized Extended Producer Responsibility Strategies to Incentivize Recovery of Single-Use Plastic Packaging Waste in Canada', *Waste Management*, 110 (2020): 20–3.
31 Eléonore Maitre-Ekern, 'Re-thinking Producer Responsibility for a Sustainable Circular Economy from Extended Producer Responsibility to Pre-market Producer Responsibility', *Journal of Cleaner Production*, 286 (2021): 125454; Walter Leal Filho, Ulla Saari, Mariia Fedoruk, et al., 'An Overview of the Problems Posed by Plastic Products and the Role of Extended Producer Responsibility in Europe', *Journal of Cleaner Production*, 214 (2019): 550–8
32 Tangpuori et al., *Talking Trash*, p. 43.
33 Diane M. Sicotte and Jessica L. Seamon, 'Solving the Plastics Problem: Moving the US from Recycling to Reduction', *Society & Natural Resources*, 34 (2021): 393–402; Maitre-Ekern, 'Re-thinking Producer Responsibility'; Leal Filho et al., 'An Overview of the Problems Posed by Plastic Products'.

34 Karen Raubenheimer and Niko Urho, 'Rethinking Global Governance of Plastics – The Role of Industry', *Marine Policy*, 113 (2020): 103802.
35 Leal Filho et al., 'An Overview of the Problems Posed by Plastic Products'.
36 Thomas Parker, 'From Plastics to the Circular Economy: What's in the European Green Deal?' *NS Packaging*, 29 January 2020, at https://www.nspackaging.com/analysis/from-plastics-to-the-circular-economy-whats-in-the-european-green-deal.
37 Megan Quinn, 'Break Free From Plastic Pollution Act Reintroduced, Plastics Industry Ramps Up Opposition', *Waste Dive*, 25 March 2021, at https://www.wastedive.com/news/break-free-from-plastic-pollution-act-reintroduced/597338.
38 Brett Nadrich, 'Comprehensive Federal Legislation Addresses the Plastic Pollution Crisis', Break Free From Plastic, 25 March 2021, at https://www.breakfreefromplastic.org/2021/03/25/comprehensive-federal-legislation-addresses-the-plastic-pollution-crisis.
39 Joshua Baca, quoted in Quinn, 'Break Free From Plastic Pollution Act Reintroduced'.
40 Carbon Tracker, *The Future's Not in Plastics*.
41 Barrowclough and Deere Birkbeck, *Transforming the Global Plastics Economy*, pp. 30–1.
42 Jakob Skovgaard and Harro van Asselt, 'The Politics of Fossil Fuel Subsidies and Their Reform: Implications for Climate Change Mitigation', *Wiley Interdisciplinary Reviews: Climate Change*, 10(4) (2019): e581; Bauer and Fontenit, 'Plastic Dinosaurs'.
43 Charles et al., *The Plastic Waste Makers Index*.
44 Alice Merry and Butch Bacani, *Unwrapping the Risks of Plastic Pollution to the Insurance Industry*, United Nations Environment Programme (UNEP), November 2019, at https://www.unepfi.org/publications/insurance-publications/psi-unwrapping-the-risks-of-plastic-pollution-to-the-insurance-industry, p. 47.
45 Charles et al., *The Plastic Waste Makers Index*, p. 13.
46 Charles et al., *The Plastic Waste Makers Index*, pp. 38–9.

47 See the discussion on the promise and peril of chemical recycling in chapter 3.

48 Saygin and Gielen, 'Zero-Emission Pathway for the Global Chemical and Petrochemical Sector', p. 16.

49 Simon et al., 'A Binding Global Agreement to Address the Life Cycle of Plastic'.

50 Azoulay et al., *Plastic and Health*.

51 Greenpeace, *Throwing Away the Future*.

52 Sergio Baffoni, 'Can Certification Save the World's Last Remaining Forests?' Environmental Paper Network, 18 March 2021, at https://environmentalpaper.org/2021/03/can-certification-save-the-worlds-last-remaining-forests.

53 Greenpeace, *Throwing Away the Future*; Christopher J. Rhodes, 'Plastic Pollution and Potential Solutions', *Science Progress*, 101(3) (2018): 207–60.

54 Rhodes, 'Plastic Pollution and Potential Solutions'.

55 Francesca De Falco, Emilia Di Pace, Mariacristina Cocca, and Maurizio Avella, 'The Contribution of Washing Processes of Synthetic Clothes to Microplastic Pollution', *Scientific Reports*, 9 (2019): 6633.

56 Simone Preuss, 'How Brands Can Transition to Pain-Free, Non-Mulesed Sheep Wool', Fashion United UK, 29 October 2019, at https://fashionunited.uk/news/business/how-brands-can-transition-to-pain-free-non-mulesed-sheep-wool/2019102945941; Terry Sim, 'AWGA Launches Merino Wool Consumer Campaign in US and UK', Sheep Central, 3 May 2021, at https://www.sheepcentral.com/awga-launches-merino-wool-consumer-campaign-in-us-and-uk/.

57 Alice Brock and Ian Williams, 'Life Cycle Assessment and Beverage Packaging', *Detritus*, 13 (2020): 47–61.

58 Holly Dove, 'Glass Packaging Forum Threatens Container Return Scheme', Greenpeace, 9 April 2021, at https://www.greenpeace.org/aotearoa/story/glass-packaging-forum-threatens-container-return-scheme.

59 See, for example, Joanne Sneddon, 'How the Wool Industry Has Undercut Itself on Mulesing', *The Conversation*, 2 May 2011, at https://theconversation.com/how-the-wool-industry-has-undercut-itself-on-mulesing-956; Oliver Munnion, 'The Capture of Policy-Making by

the Pulp and Paper Industry Is Driving Mega-Fires in Portugal and Land Grabbing in Mozambique', Environmental Paper Network, 11 January 2021, at https://environmentalpaper.org/2021/01/the-capture-of-policy-making-by-the-pulp-and-paper-industry-is-driving-mega-fires-in-portugal-and-land-grabbing-in-mozambique; Dove, 'Glass Packaging Forum Threatens Container Return Scheme'.

60   Hawkins et al., *Plastic Water*.

61   Lorraine Chow, '1 Million Plastic Bottles Bought Every Minute, That's Nearly 20,000 Every Second', *EcoWatch*, 29 June 2017, at https://www.ecowatch.com/plastic-bottle-crisis-2450299465.html.

62   Bakan, *The New Corporation*, p. 119.

63   Raul Pacheco-Vega, '(Re)theorizing the Politics of Bottled Water: Water Insecurity in the Context of Weak Regulatory Regimes', *Water*, 11(4) (2019): 658.

64   See Meikle, *American Plastic*, p. 271.

65   Naitove, 'Why "Plastic Wars" Got Me Riled'.

66   Joel Morales, 'Impact of New Plastics Regulation in China', IHS Markit, 3 February 2020, at https://ihsmarkit.com/research-analysis/impact-of-new-plastics-regulation-in-china.html.

67   Author's field notes, virtual World Petrochemical Conference, 8–12 March 2021.

68   Giorgos Kallis, Susan Paulson, Giacomo D'Alisa, and Federico Demaria, *The Case for Degrowth* (Polity, 2020); Vandana Shiva, *Soil Not Oil: Environmental Justice in a Time of Climate Crisis* (South End Press, 2008).

69   Meadows et al., *The Limits to Growth*; Giacomo D'Alisa, Federico Demaria, and Giorgos Kallis, eds, *Degrowth: A Vocabulary for a New Era* (Routledge, 2014).

70   Beatriz Rodríguez-Labajos, Ivonne Yánez, Patrick Bond, et al., 'Not So Natural An Alliance? Degrowth and Environmental Justice Movements in the Global South', *Ecological Economics*, 157 (2019): 175–84.

71   Edouard Morena, Dunja Krause, and Dimitris Stevis, eds, *Just Transitions: Social Justice in the Shift Towards a Low-Carbon World* (Pluto Press, 2020).

72 Hamilton et al., *Plastic and Climate*, pp. 87–8.
73 Tangpuori et al., *Talking Trash*, p. 37.
74 Tim Donaghy and Charlie Jiang, *Fossil Fuel Racism: How Phasing Out Oil, Gas, and Coal Can Protect Communities* (Greenpeace, Gulf Coast Center for Law & Policy, and Red Black and Green New Deal, 2021), at http://www.greenpeace.org/usa/fossil-fuel-racism, p. 5.
75 WWF et al., *The Business Case for a UN Treaty on Plastic Pollution*, p. 21.
76 Pew Charitable Trusts and SYSTEMIQ, *Breaking the Plastic Wave*, p. 17.
77 Pew Charitable Trusts and SYSTEMIQ, *Breaking the Plastic Wave*, p. 10.
78 Pew Charitable Trusts and SYSTEMIQ, *Breaking the Plastic Wave*, p. 9.
79 Solomon Hsiang, Robert Kopp, Amir Jina, et al. 'Estimating Economic Damage from Climate Change in the United States', *Science*, 356(6345) (2017): 1362–9.
80 This is discussed in more detail in chapter 4. See also Pew Charitable Trusts and SYSTEMIQ, *Breaking the Plastic Wave*, p. 44.
81 Meadows et al., *The Limits to Growth* and *Beyond the Limits*.
82 Wallace-Wells, *The Uninhabitable Earth*, p. 229.
83 Wallace-Wells, *The Uninhabitable Earth*, p. 234.
84 Author's field notes, virtual World Petrochemical Conference, 8–12 March 2021.
85 Ellen MacArthur Foundation, *Global Commitment Progress Report 2020*.
86 See the discussion on crisis in chapter 1, for example. Also Mirowski, *Never Let a Serious Crisis Go to Waste*.

Selected Readings

The History and Politics of Plastics – General

Altman, Rebecca. 2019. 'Time-Bombing the Future', *Aeon*, 2 January. Available at https://aeon.co/essays/how-20th-century-synthetics-altered-the-very-fabric-of-us-all.

Barthes, Roland. 1972. *Mythologies*. Trans. Annette Lavers. Hill and Wang.

Farrelly, Trisia, Sy Taffel, and Ian Shaw. 2021. *Plastic Legacies: Pollution, Persistence, and Politics*. Athabasca University Press.

Freinkel, Susan. 2011. *Plastic: A Toxic Love Story*. Dreamscape Media.

Gabrys, Jennifer, Gay Hawkins, and Mike Michael. 2013. *Accumulation: The Material Politics of Plastic*. Routledge.

Hawkins, Gay, Emily Potter, and Kane Race. 2015. *Plastic Water: The Social and Material Life of Bottled Water*. MIT Press.

Meikle, Jeffrey. 1995. *American Plastic*. Rutgers University Press.

Corporations and Sustainability – General

Bakan, Joel. 2020. *The New Corporation: How 'Good' Corporations Are Bad for Democracy*. Vintage Books.

Dauvergne, Peter. 2018. *Will Big Business Destroy Our Planet?* Polity.

Levy, David L. and Peter Newell. 2005. *The Business of Global Environmental Governance.* MIT Press.

Meagher, Michelle. 2020. *Competition Is Killing Us: How Big Business Is Harming Our Society and Planet – and What to Do About It.* Penguin 2020.

Ponte, Stefano. 2019. *Business, Power and Sustainability in a World of Global Value Chains.* Zed Books.

Plastics Industry and Corporate Power

Barrowclough, Diana and Carolyn Deere Birkbeck. 2020. *Transforming the Global Plastics Economy: The Political Economy and Governance of Plastics Production and Pollution.* GEG Working Paper No. 142. Available at https://www.econstor.eu/handle/10419/224117.

Clapp, Jennifer. 2012. 'The Rising Tide Against Plastic Waste: Unpacking Industry Attempts to Influence the Debate', in *Histories of the Dustheap: Waste, Material Cultures, Social Justice*, eds Stephanie Foote and Elizabeth Mazzolini. MIT Press, pp. 199–225.

Corporate Europe Observatory. 2020. 'Plastic Promises: Industry Seeking to Avoid Binding Regulations', 22 May. Available at https://corporateeurope.org/en/power-lobbies/2018/05/plastic-promises.

Eckert, Sandra. 2019. *Corporate Power and Regulation: Consumers and the Environment.* Palgrave Macmillan.

Feit, Steven. 2017. *Fuelling Plastics: Plastic Industry Awareness of the Ocean Plastics Problem.* Centre for International Environmental Law.

Gower, Rich, Joanne Green, and Mari Williams. 2020. *The Burning Question: Will Companies Reduce Their Plastic Use?* Tearfund. Available at https://learn.tearfund.org/-/media/learn/resources/reports/2020-tearfund-the-burning-question-en.pdf.

Greenpeace. 2019. *Throwing Away the Future: How Companies Still Have It Wrong on Plastic Pollution 'Solutions'*. Available at https://www.greenpeace. org/usa/research/how-companies-still-have-it-wrong-on-plastic-pollution-solutions.

Reubold, Michael, Sean Milmo, and Martin Todd. 2016. *Petrochemicals and EPCA: A Passionate Journey*. European Petrochemical Association.

Valette, Jim, et al. 2021. *The New Coal: Plastics and Climate Change*. Beyond Plastics, October. Available at https://www.beyondplastics.org/plastics-and-climate.

Plastics and Health

Azoulay, David, Priscilla Villa, Yvette Arellano, et al. 2019. *Plastic and Health: The Hidden Cost of a Plastic Planet*. Center for International Environmental Law.

Brown, Phil, Vanessa De La Rosa, and Alissa Cordner. 2020. 'Toxic Trespass: Science, Activism, and Policy Concerning Chemicals in Our Bodies', in *Toxic Truths: Environmental Justice and Citizen Science in a Post-Truth Age*, eds Thom Davies and Alice Mah. Manchester University Press, pp. 34–58.

Markowitz, Gerald E., and David Rosner. 2002. *Deceit and Denial: The Deadly Politics of Industrial Pollution*. University of California Press.

Michaels, David. 2008. *Doubt Is their Product: How Industry's Assault on Science Threatens Your Health*. Oxford University Press.

Mudu, Pierpaolo, Benedetto Terracini, and Marco Martuzzi, eds. 2014. *Human Health in Areas with Industrial Contamination*. WHO Regional Office for Europe.

Plastics, Fossil Fuels, and Climate

Banerjee, Neela, John H. Cushman Jr, David Hasemyer, and Lisa Song. 2015. *Exxon: The Road Not Taken*.

Inside Climate News. Available at https://insideclimate
news.org/book/exxon-the-road-not-taken.

Carbon Tracker. 2020. *The Future's Not in Plastics:
Why Plastics Sector Demand Won't Rescue the Oil
Sector*, 4 September. Available at: https://carbon
tracker.org/reports/the-futures-not-in-plastics.

Charles, Dominic, Laurent Kimman, and Nakul Saran,
2021. *The Plastic Waste Makers Index*, Minderoo
Foundation.

Donaghy, Tim and Charlie Jiang. 2021. *Fossil Fuel
Racism: How Phasing Out Oil, Gas, and Coal
Can Protect Communities*. Greenpeace, Gulf Coast
Center for Law & Policy, and Red Black and Green
New Deal. Available at: http://www.greenpeace.org/
usa/fossil-fuel-racism.

Hamilton, Lisa A., Steven Feit, Carroll Muffett, et al.
2019. *Plastic and Climate: The Hidden Costs of a
Plastic Planet*. Center for International Environmental
Law.

Klein, Naomi. 2014. *This Changes Everything:
Capitalism Versus the Climate*. Simon & Schuster.

Oreskes, Naomi and Erik M. Conway. 2011. *Merchants
of Doubt: How a Handful of Scientists Obscured
the Truth on Issues from Tobacco Smoke to Global
Warming*. Bloomsbury.

Tong, David. 2020. *Big Oil Reality Check*. Oil Change
International.

Wallace-Wells, David. 2019. *The Uninhabitable Earth:
A Story of the Future*. Penguin.

Wylie, Sara Ann. 2018. *Fractivism: Corporate Bodies
and Chemical Bonds*. Duke University Press.

Plastics and the Circular Economy

Ellen MacArthur Foundation. 2017. *The New Plastics
Economy: Rethinking the Future of Plastics &
Catalysing Action*. Ellen MacArthur Foundation, with
support from the World Economic Forum. Available

at   https://www.ellenmacarthurfoundation.org/
publications/the-new-plastics-economy-rethinking-
the-future-of-plastics-catalysing-action.
European Commission. 2018. *European Strategy for Plastics in a Circular Economy.*

Marine Plastics Crisis
Cirino, Erica. 2021. *Thicker Than Water: The Quest for Solutions to the Plastic Crisis.* Island Press.
Dauvergne, Peter. 2018. 'Why is the Global Governance of Plastic Failing the Oceans?' *Global Environmental Change*, 51: 22–31.
Eriksen, Marcus. 2017. *Junk Raft: An Ocean Voyage and a Rising Tide of Activism to Fight Plastic Pollution.* Beacon Press.
Mendenhall, Elizabeth. 2018. 'Oceans of Plastic: A Research Agenda to Propel Policy Development', *Marine Policy*, 96: 291–8.
Pew Charitable Trusts and SYSTEMIQ. 2020. *Breaking the Plastic Wave: A Comprehensive Assessment of Pathways Towards Stopping Ocean Pollution.*
Siegle, Lucy. 2018. *Turning the Tide on Plastic: How Humanity (And You) Can Make Our Globe Clean Again.* Orion Publishing.
Smith, Jesse and Sasha Vignieri, eds. 2021. Special Issue: 'Our Plastics Dilemma', *Science*, 373(6550).

Plastics, Waste, and Recycling
Altman, Rebecca. 2021. 'On Wishcycling', *Discard Studies*, 15 February. Available at https://discard studies.com/2021/02/15/on-wishcycling.
Goldstein, Joshua. 2020. *Remains of the Everyday: A Century of Recycling in Beijing.* University of California Press.
MacBride, Samantha. 2011. *Recycling Reconsidered: The Present Failure and Future Promise of Environmental Action in the United States.* MIT Press.

Minter, Adam. 2013. *Junkyard Planet: Travels in the Billion-Dollar Trash Trade.* Bloomsbury.

O'Neill, Kate. 2019. *Waste.* Polity.

Strausser, Susan. 2000. *Waste and Want: A Social History of Trash.* Holt.

Environmental Justice and Plastic Pollution

Calil, Juliano, Marce Gutiérrez-Graudiņš, Steffanie Munguía, and Christopher Chin. 2021. *Neglected Environmental Justice Impacts of Marine Litter and Plastic Pollution.* UNEP.

Global Alliance for Incinerator Alternatives. 2019. *Discarded: Communities on the Frontlines of the Global Plastic Crisis.*

Greenpeace. 2021. *Trashed: How the UK Is Still Dumping Plastic Trash on the Rest of the World.* Available at https://www.greenpeace.org.uk/ resources/trashed-plastic-report.

Liamson, Catherine, Sherma Benosa, Miko Aliño, and Beau Baconguis. 2020. *Sachet Economy: Big Problems in Small Packets.* Global Alliance for Incinerator Alternatives.

Liboiron, Max. 2021. *Pollution Is Colonialism.* Duke University Press.

Pellow, David N. 2007. *Resisting Global Toxics: Transnational Movements for Environmental Justice.* MIT Press.

Wiebe, Sara M. 2016. *Everyday Exposure: Indigenous Mobilization and Environmental Justice in Canada's Chemical Valley.* UBC Press.

Plastics and the Pandemic

DeBlasio, Nicola and Phoebe Fallon. 2021. *Avoiding a Plastic Pandemic: The Future of Sustainability in a Post COVID-19 World.* Belfer Center for Science and International Affairs, Harvard Kennedy School.

Dey, Tridibesh and Mike Michael. 2020. 'Driving

Home "Single-Use": Plastic Politics in the Times of the COVID-19', *Discover Society*, 30 April. Available at: https://discoversociety.org/2020/04/30/driving-home-single-use-plastic-politics-in-the-times-of-the-covid-19.

Schlegel, Ian and Connor Gibson. 2020. 'The Making of an Echo Chamber: How the Plastic Industry Exploited Anxiety About COVID-19 to Attack Reusable Bags'. Greenpeace. Available at: https://www.greenpeace.org/usa/research/how-the-plastic-industry-exploited-anxiety-about-covid-19.

Tangpuori, Alice Delemare, George Harding-Rolls, Nusa Urbancic, and Ximena Purita Banegas Zallio. 2021. *Talking Trash: The Corporate Playbook of False Solutions to the Plastics Crisis*. Changing Markets Foundation.

Plastic-Free Lifestyles

Dorey, Martin. 2018. *No. More. Plastic.: What You Can Do to Make a Difference – the #2minutesolution*. Penguin.

McCallum, Will. 2018. *How to Give Up Plastic: A Guide to Changing the World, One Plastic Bottle at a Time*. Penguin.

The F Team. 2018. *F**k Plastic: 101 Ways to Free Yourself from Plastic and Save the World*. Seven Dials.

Degrowth and the Limits to Growth

D'Alisa, Giacomo, Federico Demaria, and Giorgos Kallis, eds. 2014. *Degrowth: A Vocabulary for a New Era*. Routledge.

Hickel, Jason, 2020. *Less Is More: How Degrowth Will Save the World*. Random House.

Jackson, Tim, 2021. *Post Growth: Life After Capitalism*. Polity.

Kallis, George, Susan Paulson, Giacomo D'Alisa, and

Federico Demaria. 2020. *The Case for Degrowth.* Polity.

Meadows, Donella, Jørgen Randers, and Dennis Meadows. 2004. *Limits to Growth: The 30-Year Update.* Chelsea Green Publishing.

Index